WATER WAS NOT TURNED INTO WINE

HENRY LOUIS GREEN

authorHOUSE®

AuthorHouse™
1663 Liberty Drive
Bloomington, IN 47403
www.authorhouse.com
Phone: 1 (800) 839-8640

Published by AuthorHouse   03/07/2016

ISBN: 978-1-5049-8153-8 (sc)
ISBN: 978-1-5049-8152-1 (e)

Library of Congress Control Number: 2016903374

Print information available on the last page.

Any people depicted in stock imagery provided by Thinkstock are models,
and such images are being used for illustrative purposes only.
Certain stock imagery © Thinkstock.

This book is printed on acid-free paper.

Because of the dynamic nature of the Internet, any web addresses or links contained in
this book may have changed since publication and may no longer be valid. The views
expressed in this work are solely those of the author and do not necessarily reflect the
views of the publisher, and the publisher hereby disclaims any responsibility for them.

KJV
Scripture quotations marked KJV are from the Holy Bible, King James Version
(Authorized Version). First published in 1611. Quoted from the KJV Classic
Reference Bible, Copyright © 1983 by The Zondervan Corporation.

THIS BOOK IS DEDICATED TO ALL

THE PEOPLE

OF THE WORLD

Because.......

"The earth is the Lord's, and the fullness thereof;
the world, and they that dwell therein."
Psalm 24:1 KJV

"Seventy years [ago] Henry Louis Green of Mitchellville, a retired 94-year-old landscaper, began writing his first book, "Water Was Not Turned Into Wine," and [now it is finally published,] said Serita G. Newell of Upper Marlboro, Green's youngest daughter and his writing assistant."

The Gazette, Thursday, August 29, 2013,
Prince Georges County, MD

Contents

Illustrative Artwork by Kennedy Jasmine Ringgold

**Drawing of Henry Louis Green, when he
began the book at age 21 and at age 75.**

Preface

After seventy years a new author, at age 96, Henry Louis Green of Mitchellville, Md., is finally finished with his book, "Water Was Not Turned Into Wine," with the assistance of his youngest daughter, Serita G. Newell of Upper Marlboro, Md. "Water Was Not Turned Into Wine" is a book that looks at what some would call Jesus' first miracle and the consequences and ill effects of alcohol. Henry could not complete his book sooner because he was such a devoted husband and father. To the author, family comes first. After the death of his loving wife, Marion in 2011, he decided to devote more time to his writing.

Henry would take time out to write, sometimes sitting in the garage or in the backyard on a summer evening after working in his vegetable garden. The author said he would just write a little bit at a time, each day depending on how his spirit was, and then he would write because that's the way life goes. The author has been writing throughout his life and has six other books in the works, however, he would like to get his first book published and get feedback from everyone before getting the others published.

Henry is the father of four sons, Robert Henry, Lorenzo Louis, Ted William and Carroll Brent Green and two daughters, Priscilla

G. Francis and Serita G. Newell. His children are gratified to see him materialize all his hard work. The author said he has experienced a full life already, from growing up on a plantation to raising six children. Four of the six children were raised in South Boston, Va. After the birth of the last two children, the author moved the family in the late 60s to start a new life in Washington, D.C. and after retirement he moved to Maryland, where he remains until today.

This year, the author will be 97 years young and his days consist of riding his stationary bike twice a day, and growing vegetables in his backyard, singing at Crossover Church on senior Sunday, cooking soups and writing.

Recently God revealed to him that he should dedicate the book to, "All The People of the World," because the Bible says, "The earth is the Lord's, and the fullness thereof; the world, and they that dwell therein. Psalm 24:1 KJV

Introduction

"In the beginning was the Word, and the Word
was with God, and the Word was God."
John 1:1 King James Version

"And the Word was made flesh, and dwelt among
us, (and we beheld his glory, the glory as of the only
begotten of the Father,) full of grace and truth."
John 1:14 King James Version (KJV)

"So shall MY word be that goeth forth out of
MY mouth: it shall not return unto ME void, but
it shall accomplish that which I please, and it
shall prosper in the thing whereto I sent it."
Isaiah 55:11 King James Version (KJV)

The Bible, "the written word of God," is the sacred Holy Book which I have read and learned valuable lessons for living my daily Christian life. Over the years, I have searched and studied the scriptures, and have applied the lessons learned in my daily life. The more I read the Bible the better my understanding of its teachings became. The Bible teaches us to, "Study to show thy self approved unto God, a workman that need not to be ashamed, rightly dividing the word of truth." 2 Timothy 2:15. Also, in the Bible, "Jesus answered and said unto them, Ye do err, not knowing the scriptures, nor the power of God." Matthew 22:29 Jeremiah, the prophet, said, "And ye shall seek me, and find me, when ye shall search for me with all your heart. And I will be found of you, saith the LORD:" (Jeremiah 29:13-14, King James Version (KJV))

My book, "Water Was Not Turned Into Wine" is about whether the Christ actually turned water into wine at the wedding at Cana and what the Bible says concerning wine and strong drink.

It has been over 70 years ago, when at a Bible study session at church, it was brought to my attention that water was not turned into wine at, "the wedding at Cana." St. John 2:1-11. I want to share my understanding of what the Bible says about water not turned into wine and how wine or strong drink can affect your life and the world. These thoughts hung heavy on my heart because so many individuals and families have suffered, and lives have been destroyed because of the abuse of alcohol. Husbands and wives are abusing their spouses and children. Young children are also abusing their bodies using alcohol and are becoming alcoholics. Many lives are lost due to drinking while driving. Alcohol abuse has lead to violent deaths by guns and other devises. Such abuse can also lead to the demise of individuals through cirrhosis of the liver and other diseases.

The Bible is read all around the world and people believe and respect what is said in the Bible. If people understand that water was not turned into wine by Jesus, and that according to scriptures in the Bible, drinking wine and strong drink can have a devastating effect on your life, then maybe the world will change its view about wine and strong drink being so acceptable. Alcohol is glorified and glamorized in the movies and through advertisers who spend over $400 million each year. However, the Bible says, "Wine is a mocker, and strong drink is raging: and whosoever is deceived thereby is not wise." Proverbs 20:1

In view of the above, I think it is absolutely imperative that I show through scripture in the Bible, that water was not turned into wine during the wedding at Cana. I will also refer to other verses in the Bible which I believe send a message to everyone about the warnings and consequences of misusing wine and strong drink. In Chapter I, you will read the exact details of what happened at the "wedding at Cana" and, if you look closely, it will be revealed to you that the governor of the feast who made the claim about what was in the cups must have been mistaken.

The Bible is also full of inspirational teachings that I would encourage all Christians to emulate in order to live a more abundant "Christ centered" life. In reading "Water Not Turned Into Wine," I hope you will begin to understand some of the many lessons from the Bible. You will also learn that in other scriptures which mention, "…. fruit of the vine" the Bible did not necessarily mean wine. For example, in Matthew 7:20, Jesus said, "Wherefore by their fruits ye shall know them"; this is not a reference to wine, instead it refers to the test of a person's character, which is not determined by their outward appearance but though their deeds. When God said, "Be fruitful and multiply" in Genesis 1:28, He was referring to replenishing the earth by having many children. In John 15:5, Jesus said, "I am the vine, ye are the branches: He that abideth in me, and I in him, the same bringeth forth much fruit: for without me ye can do nothing."(John 15:5 KJV) At the time Jesus was referring to Himself as the vine, a source of life and His twelve disciples were the branches. In this manner, the disciples were commissioned by the Christ to spread the gospel about God. Christ also commissioned them to lead the people (or "the fruit") to salvation because without Him there is no spiritual life or hope of eternal reward.

I would encourage everyone to read the rich Holy Scriptures of the Bible because they are full of powerful lessons that will enrich your lives. Moreover, not reading the Bible can leave you spiritually poorer. Yet, there is still an answer and hope for those who are spiritually poor because the Bible says, in Matthew 5:3, "Blessed are the poor in spirit: for theirs is the kingdom of heaven."

Chapter 1

"The Wedding At Cana"

The Gospel According to St. John 2:1-11

Although Chapter 2 of St. John is about the "Wedding at Cana," I thought it best to give you a little background about what important events occurred in Chapter 1 before the wedding. The Gospel According to St. John was written by John the Beloved who also wrote the Book of Revelation. In the first chapter of St. John, John the Beloved wrote about John the Baptist because he (John the Baptist) baptized Jesus. John the Baptist was amazed by Jesus even from the womb of his mother and even more after baptizing Him.

John the Baptist was a very special person in the Bible. John the Baptist's mother, Elizabeth, was a relative of Mary, the mother of Jesus. The two women were pregnant at the same time and both were forbidden to drink wine. The Bible says in Luke 1:41, when the two expectant mothers met, the baby leaped within Elizabeth's womb as she was filled with the Holy Spirit.

Luke 1:41-42

41 And it came to pass, that, when Elisabeth heard the salutation of Mary, the babe leaped in her womb; and Elisabeth was filled with the Holy Ghost:

42 And she spake out with a loud voice, and said, Blessed art thou among women, and blessed is the fruit of thy womb.

John the Baptist was born to bear witness to the coming of Jesus and to baptize Jesus at the appropriate time.

John 1:6-8

6 There was a man sent from God, whose name was John.

7 The same came for a witness, to bear witness of the Light, that all men through him might believe.

8 He was not that Light, but was sent to bear witness of that Light.

According to John's Gospel (St. John 1:35-39), the day after Jesus was baptized, several of His followers began their discipleship. Also, according to this passage, the first to follow Him was Andrew who made that decision after hearing John the Baptist declare that Jesus was the Lamb of God. According to Mark, after Jesus was baptized by John the Baptist, "Immediately the Spirit driveth him into the wilderness. And He was there in the wilderness forty days, tempted by Satan, and was with the wild beasts; and the angels ministered unto him." (Mark 1:12-13 KJV) Also Matthew and Luke agree with Mark that Jesus went into the desert and fasted for forty days and nights, where He was tempted by the Devil. Although St. John does not speak of the temptation of Christ during the 40 days and nights fast, Mark, Luke, and Matthew agree that it occurred after the baptism of Jesus. Therefore, the order in which these significant events occurred is: 1) the <u>Baptism of Jesus in the Jordan river by John the Baptist</u>; 2) <u>first disciple, Andrew decides to follow Jesus</u> after hearing He was the Lamb of God; 3) <u>Jesus goes into the wilderness (Judean desert) and fasts for 40 days and nights,</u> and, there He was tempted by the Devil (again, this event is not found in St. John.); and 4) <u>Jesus attends the wedding at Cana in Galilee</u> (according to St. John – notably, this event is not mentioned in Mark, Matthew, or Luke). However, all of these writers agree that Jesus was baptized by John the Baptist and the baptism of Jesus was a significant event and the beginning of his public ministry. The <u>Baptism</u> is one of five major events in the life of Jesus, the others being the Transfiguration, Crucifixion, Resurrection, and Ascension.

In Chapter 1 of the Gospel According to St. John 1:1-2 and verse 14 and 23, it states the following about the Christ:

> 1 In the beginning was the Word, and the Word was with God, and the Word was God.

> 2 The same was in the beginning with God. [Ref. to Genesis]

14 And the Word was made flesh, and dwelt among us, (and we beheld his glory, the glory as of the only begotten of the Father,) full of grace and truth.

23 He said, I am the voice of one [referring to John the Baptist] crying in the wilderness, Make straight the way of the LORD, as said the prophet Esaias.

Also, in St. John 1:29-33, it states the following about John the Baptist:

29 The next day John seeth Jesus coming unto him, and saith, Behold the Lamb of God, which taketh away the sin of the world. 30 This is He of whom I said, After me cometh a man which is preferred before me: for He was before me. 31 And I knew Him not: but that He should be made manifest to Israel, therefore am I come baptizing with water. 32 And John bare record, saying, I saw the Spirit descending from heaven like a dove, and it abode upon Him. 33 And I knew Him not: but He that sent me to baptize with water, the same said unto me, Upon whom thou shalt see the Spirit descending, and remaining on Him, the same is He which baptizeth with the Holy Ghost. 34 And I saw, and bare record that this is the Son of God. 35 Again the next day after John stood, and two of his disciples; 36 And looking upon Jesus as He walked, He saith, Behold the Lamb of God!

Then Jesus says to John the Baptist according to St. John 1:51, "And He saith unto him, Verily, verily, I say unto you, Hereafter ye shall see heaven open, and the angels of God ascending and descending upon the Son of man." In St. Matthew, he said something similar to St. John, Matthew states, "And Jesus, when He was baptized, went up straightway out of the water: and, lo, the heavens were opened unto him, and he saw the Spirit of God descending like a dove, and lighting upon Him: And lo a voice from heaven, saying, This is my beloved Son, in whom I am well pleased." Matthew 3:16-17 St Mark agreed with Matthew about the heavens opening up and a voice came from heaven, saying, "Thou art MY beloved Son, in whom I am well pleased." St. Mark 1:11 Luke also witnessed the same events of the heavens opening up and a voice speaking from heaven. According to St. Matthew 3:16-17 and 4:1-11, St. Mark 1:10-13, or St Luke 3:22 and 4:1-4, after Jesus was baptized by John the Baptist, then Jesus who was full of the Holy Ghost was led up by the Spirit into the wilderness and fasted for forty day and nights and was tempted by the devil.

St. John followed Jesus waiting for more signs and wonders. And then after everything above happened, St. John witnessed Jesus recruiting some of His disciples [Andrew, Simon Peter's brother and Simon whom Jesus called Cephas]. However after the baptism, St. John did not mention God's voice from heaven or Jesus immediately going into the wilderness and fasting for forty days and nights, like three other witnesses, Matthew, Mark and Luke. Instead, St. John's Chapter 2, he describes a wedding in which Jesus attends and He begins by saying "And the third day there was a marriage in Cana of Galilee; and the mother of Jesus was there." The Bible states the following about The Wedding at Cana:

THE WEDDING AT CANA
St. John 2:1-11

1 And the third day there was a marriage in Cana of Galilee; and the mother of Jesus was there:

2 And both Jesus was called, and his disciples, to the marriage.

3 And when they wanted wine, the mother of Jesus saith unto him, They have no wine.

4 Jesus saith unto her, Woman, what have I to do with thee? mine hour is not yet come.

5 His mother saith unto the servants, Whatsoever He saith unto you, do it.

6 And there were set there six waterpots of stone, after the manner of the purifying of the Jews, containing two or three firkins apiece.

7 Jesus saith unto them, Fill the waterpots with water. And they filled them up to the brim.

8 And He saith unto them, Draw out now, and bear unto the governor of the feast. And they bare it.

9 When the ruler of the feast had tasted the water that was made wine, and knew not whence it was: (but the servants which drew the water knew;) the governor of the feast called the bridegroom,

10 And saith unto him, Every man at the beginning doth set forth good wine; and when men have well drunk, then that which is worse: but thou hast kept the good wine until now.

11 This beginning of miracles [or "signs" in the Jerusalem Bible] did Jesus in Cana of Galilee, and manifested forth his glory; and his disciples believed on him.

As you can see from the verses above, only "the servants which drew the water knew:" and that the governor who "knew not whence it was (St. John 2:9)," said it was wine. However, only the servant who drew the water knew. The Bible says, "Wine is a mocker, strong drink is raging: and whosoever is deceived thereby is not wise." (Prov. 20:1) What is the opposite of wise? The Bible also says in Leviticus 10:9-10, "9 Do not drink wine nor strong drink, thou, nor thy sons with thee, when ye go into the tabernacle of the congregation, lest ye die: it shall be a statute for ever throughout your generations: 10 And that ye may put difference between holy and unholy, and between unclean and clean;" (Leviticus 10:9-10) Also, at Judges 13:4, 7, 14, "4 Now therefore beware, I pray thee, and drink not wine nor strong drink, and eat not any unclean thing:" "7 But he said unto me, Behold, thou shalt conceive, and bear a son; and now drink no wine nor strong drink, neither eat any unclean thing: for the child (Samson) shall be a Nazarite to God from the womb to the day of his death." "14 She (Manoah, mother of Samson) may not eat of anything that cometh of the vine, neither let her drink wine or strong drink, nor eat any unclean thing: all that I commanded her let her observe." This gives further evidence that wine or strong drink is not good for you, especially pregnant women. The Bible says in Matthew 22:29, "Ye do err, not knowing the scriptures, nor the power of God."

In Matthew 23:24, it states, "Ye blind guides, which strain at a gnat, and swallow a camel." In other words, we make a big deal about small things and let the big things get by us. In the Bible, at Isaiah 35:8, it says, "And a highway shall be there, and a way, and it shall be called the way of holiness; the unclean shall not pass over it; but it shall be for those: the wayfaring men, though fools, shall not err therein. God's way of life is like "a highway" and therefore it should be so plain that even "the wayfaring men, though fools, shall not err therein." In Timothy 2:15, the Bible says, "Study to shew thyself approved unto God, a workman that needeth not to be ashamed, rightly dividing the word of truth." In Matthew 7:13-14, "13 Enter ye in at the strait gate: for wide is the gate, and broad is the way, that leadeth to destruction, and many there be which go in thereat: 14 Because strait is the gate, and narrow is the way, which leadeth unto life, and few there be that find it." The way to destruction is easily accessible and most people go that route versus the narrower way which very few are able to find (that is, the clean and Godly life). So therefore, if you read closely the scripture, and rightly divide the word of God, you see that no one except the servants knew what was in the vases. In Isaiah 28:7, it states, "7 But they also have erred through wine, and through strong drink are out of the way; the priest and the prophet have erred through strong drink, they are swallowed up of wine, they are out of the way through strong drink; they err in vision, they stumble in judgment." The priests were warned as early as Leviticus <u>not to drink wine and strong drink</u>.

According to the Luke 1:13-15, "13 But the angel said unto him, Fear not, Zacharias: for thy prayer is heard; and thy wife Elisabeth shall bear thee a son, and thou shalt call his name John (the Baptist). 14 And thou shalt have joy and gladness; and many shall rejoice at his birth. 15 For he shall be great in the sight of the LORD, and <u>shall drink neither wine nor strong drink</u>; and he shall be filled with the Holy Ghost, even from his mother's womb.

The Bible said in John 2:9, "the servants which drew the water knew:" and that the governor who "knew not whence it was," said it was wine. According to the Bible, pregnant women in the Bible, such as, Samson's mother and John the Baptist mother, were <u>forbidden to drink wine or strong drink</u>. Based on the examination of scripture above, Christ could not have turned water into wine at the "Wedding at Cana".

In the Bible, Jesus said, "I have glorified thee on earth: I have finished the work which thou gavest me to do."(John 17:4) This means Christ came here to finish the work that the Father gave Him to do; therefore, at the wedding He knew that doing what His mother, Mary had asked of him was not timely. We know this because of what He told his mother, "Woman, what have I to do with thee? Mine hour is not yet come." (St. John 2:4) This was not the first time Jesus had chided His mother. When Jesus was only 12 years old, His parents traveled to Jerusalem for the Feast of the Passover. The Bible says in Luke 2:40, "And the child grew, and waxed strong in spirit, filled with wisdom and grace of God was upon Him." So even at a very young age He was, "filled with wisdom and grace of God." Luke 2:40 On this occasion, after the feast was over, Jesus stayed behind, however, His parents had been looking Him for three days and were worried.

The Bible says in Luke 2:40-52 KJV the following about what happened after The Feast of the Passover:

> 40 And the child grew, and waxed strong in spirit, filled with wisdom: and the grace of God was upon him.

> 41 Now his parents went to Jerusalem every year at the feast of the passover.

> 42 And when he was twelve years old, they went up to Jerusalem after the custom of the feast.

43 And when they had fulfilled the days, as they returned, the child Jesus tarried behind in Jerusalem; and Joseph and his mother knew not of it.

44 But they, supposing him to have been in the company, went a day's journey; and they sought him among their kinsfolk and acquaintance.

45 And when they found him not, they turned back again to Jerusalem, seeking him.

46 And it came to pass, that after three days they found him in the temple, sitting in the midst of the doctors, both hearing them, and asking them questions.

47 And all that heard him were astonished at his understanding and answers.

48 And when they saw him, they were amazed: and his mother said unto him, Son, why hast thou thus dealt with us? behold, thy father and I have sought thee sorrowing.

49 And he said unto them, How is it that ye sought me? wist ye not that I must be about my Father's business?

50 And they understood not the saying which he spake unto them.

51 And he went down with them, and came to Nazareth, and was subject unto them: but his mother kept all these sayings in her heart.

52 And Jesus increased in wisdom and stature, and in favour with God and man.

In this instance, Jesus was found in the temple, sitting in the midst of the doctors, both hearing them, and asking them questions wherein they were astonished at his understanding and answers. Luke 2:46 Then in Luke 2:47, Jesus mother and others who had been looking for Him found Him and His mother said, "Son, why hast thou thus dealt with us" behold, thy [earthly] father [Joseph] and I have sought thee sorrowing. Then Jesus chided His mother by saying, "How is it that ye sought Me wist ye not that I must be about My Father's business?" Luke 2:49 According to the Bible, Christ was here on earth on a mission to do the work of His Father before dying on the cross for our sins. Although Mary did not understand what He was saying, she kept all these sayings in her heart. Luke 2:51

Even at the young age of 12, He was wise beyond His years and He found "favour with God and man." Luke 2:52 Now as an adult He is even more wise and He finds Himself at a wedding before His appointed hour. He attends the "Wedding at Cana" and His mother made an unexpected request of Him. He then gave instructions to the servants to "Fill the water pots with water. And they filled them up to the brim," (St. John 2:8), however only the servants knew what was in the water pots not the Governor. (St. John 2:9) Had Jesus Christ turned water into wine, He would have totally disregarded the biblical warning (Habakkuk 2:15) which says, "Woe unto him that giveth his neighbour drink, that puttest thy bottle to him, and makest him drunken also. . ." And, if Jesus disobeyed Habakkuk, He would have been a sinner! The Bible makes it very clear that Jesus was without sin in 1 Peter 2:22-24 and 2 Corinthians 5:21:

1 Peter 2:21-24

> 21 For even hereunto were ye called: because Christ also suffered for us, leaving us an example, that ye should follow his steps:

> 22 Who did no sin, neither was guile found in his mouth:

> 23 Who, when He was reviled, reviled not again; when He suffered, He threatened not; but committed himself to him that judgeth righteously:

> 24 Who His own self bare our sins in His own body on the tree, that we, being dead to sins, should live unto righteousness: by whose stripes ye were healed.

2 Corinthians 5:20-21

> 20 Now then we are ambassadors for Christ, as though God did beseech you by us: we pray you in Christ's stead, be ye reconciled to God.

21 For HE hath made Him to be sin for us, who knew no sin; that we might be made the righteousness of God in Him.

Why did John decide to record this event? It is not recorded in any other place in the Bible or the synoptic gospels. John did not view it as a miracle. He viewed it as a sign, not a miracle. In John 2:11 of the Jerusalem Bible, John says, "This was the first sign given by Jesus...." John knew the people needed proof because "every true prophet must have 'signs', or wonders worked in God's name." (Isa 7:11, cited in the Jerusalem Bible, John 2:11, footnote f.) The circumstances and sequence of events of the wedding at Cana, and of water being turned into wine, have been discussed by many for many years. Was there an actual transformation or changing of water into wine, or was this a spiritual allegory in which "the good wine" could be interpreted as the Christ Himself? To answer these questions consider the following:

On the third day, Jesus, His disciples, and His mother attended a wedding at Cana in the city of Galilee. At the wedding a situation came up where they were running out of wine. Mary, Jesus' mother, thought Jesus could solve the problem and gave specific instructions to the servants to do whatever He said. Jesus, who seemed annoyed at first, after a few chiding words, appears to acquiesce to his mother's request. Nearby stood six stone water jars, the kind used by the Jews for ceremonial washing and each could hold between twenty to thirty gallons or a total of 120 to 180 gallons. He then gave specific instruction to the servants to fill the jars with water and they filled them to the brim. The Governor of the feast tasted it, but didn't know where it came from, and then said to the bridegroom, "Every man at the beginning doth set forth good wine; and when men have well drunk, then that which is worse: but thou hast kept the good wine until now."

In an internet article from stjudechapel.org entitled, "Pilgrimage to the Holy Land: The Marriage at Cana," regarding the Governor's statement about saving the good wine for last, it states, "This could be interpreted by saying simply that it is always darkest before the dawn, but good things are on the way." The more usual interpretation, however, is that this is a reference to the **appearance of Jesus**, whom the author of the Fourth Gospel regards as being Himself, the good wine." John later records in Chapter 10:10, that Jesus said, "The thief cometh not, but for to steal, and to kill, and to destroy: I am come that they might have life, and that they might have it more abundantly." Jesus wants us to have a more abundant life. How can we have a more abundant life if we believe Jesus turned water into wine? We cannot give credence to what the Governor (who was probably drunk) said about "the good wine" because he didn't even know where it came from. However, based on all the biblical scriptures I have cited about wine and strong drink (here and in Chapter II), it does not strain reason to conclude that water was not turned into wine at the wedding at Cana. Moreover, as an allegory, it is probably best to interpret **the actual appearance of Jesus at this wedding**

as saving the best for last. I say this because, realistically, why would Jesus want to give wine (120 or 180 gallons) to people who were already drunk? Also, consider everything that happened prior to the wedding at Cana. Consider 1) the <u>Baptism of Jesus in the Jordan river by John the Baptist</u> (where the "Spirit descending from heaven like a dove, and it abode upon him" St. John 1:32), 2) <u>Jesus goes into the wilderness (Judean desert) and fasted for 40 days and nights</u> where He was tempted by the Devil. 3) The <u>first of 12 disciples, Andrew decides to follow Jesus</u> after hearing He was the Lamb of God.

Wherever Jesus went the people were changed; such as two men fishing became fishers of men, He found Lazarus dead and left him alive, He made the blind to see, He saved the unsaved, unable to walk and Jesus made them walk. It is no wonder that Jesus became famous throughout Syria when He went about all of Galilee, teaching in their synagogues, and preaching the gospel of the kingdom and healing all manner of sickness and disease among the people and they brought unto Him all sick people with diseases, torments, possessed with devils, mentally sick, palsy; and He healed them. Then as Isaiah, a prophet in the Old Testament prophesied that the Messiah (Jesus Christ), would be an offspring of Jesse, the father of David and that the spirit of the LORD shall rest upon Him, the spirit of wisdom and understanding, the spirit of counsel and might, the spirit of knowledge and of the fear of the LORD and that with righteousness shall He judge the poor, and reprove with equity for the meek of the earth: and He shall smite the earth: with the rod of his mouth, and with the breath of his lips shall He slay the wicked. (Isaiah 11:2-3 KJV) Jesus used all of these spiritual gifts when He gave his famous Sermon on the Mount. (See Chapter VI of this book, "The Sermon On The Mount," which include The Beatitudes, Matthew 5-7, KJV)

After all of those events above which (which according to Matthew, Mark and Luke) more than likely happened before the wedding, you can understand why St. John was following Jesus. Furthermore, only St. John presents a record of the wedding where Jesus, the Lamb of God (St. John also described Him as the Son of God, Light of the World, Bread of Life and Life of the World), his mother and his disciples are in attendance (here again, neither Matthew, Mark, nor Luke recorded the wedding). St. John recorded the wedding because Jesus was there and he was looking for a sign. Perhaps Jesus told the servants to fill the stone pots with water because the people needed to sober up so they could hear some good news, such as that found in St. John 4:14, when Jesus said, "But whosoever drinketh of the water that I shall give him shall never thirst; but the water that I shall give him shall be in him a well of water springing up into everlasting life." Jesus told the Samaritan woman at the well, "But whosoever drinketh of the water that I shall give him shall never thirst; but the water that I shall give him shall be in him a well of water springing up into everlasting life." (John 4:14 KJV) Don't let the Devil's version (for "The thief cometh not, but for to steal, and to kill, and to destroy….," John 10:10) of what happened at the wedding deter you from the truth that water was not turned into wine.

Finally, God has placed a very strong warning in 1 Corinthians 6:9-10, "Be not deceived: . . . no drunkards . . . shall inherit the kingdom of God." In Ephesians 5:18-22, it says, at verse 18 And be not drunk with wine, wherein is excess; but be filled with the Spirit; 19 Speaking to yourselves in psalms and hymns and spiritual songs, singing and making melody in your heart to the LORD; 20 Giving thanks always for all things unto God and the Father in the name of our Lord Jesus Christ. The Bible also teaches, "Be sober, be vigilant; because your adversary the devil, as a roaring lion, walketh about, seeking whom he may devour." 1 Peter 5:8. I strongly believe and the Bible teaches, "My people are destroyed for lack of knowledge." Hosea 4:6 The Bible also teaches that "Wisdom is the principal thing; therefore get wisdom: and with all thy getting get understanding." Proverbs 4:7 The Bible says, "And you will know the truth, and the truth will <u>make</u> you free." John 8:32 Therefore, "When the Spirit of truth comes, he will guide you into all the truth, for he will not speak on his own authority, but whatever he hears he will speak, and he will declare to you the things that are to come." John 16:13 And finally, the Bible says, in Colossians, "And let the peace of God rule in your hearts, to the which also ye are called in one body; and be ye thankful. Let the word of Christ dwell in you richly in all wisdom; teaching and admonishing one another in psalms and hymns and spiritual songs, singing with grace in your hearts to the LORD. And whatsoever ye do in word or deed, do all in the name of the Lord Jesus, giving thanks to God and the Father by him." (Colossians 3:15-17 (KJV)

Chapter II

"Wine is a Mocker"

As you can see from the previous chapter, there is definitely a contradiction and to further emphasize why wine and strong drink is not wise, the Bible does teach total abstinence from alcohol. The Bible says alcoholic drink or strong drink is evil. It is not just the amount one drinks that makes drinking a sin, God condemns the drink itself. The Bible teaches, "Wine is a mocker, strong drink is raging: and whosoever is deceived thereby is not wise." (Prov 20:1 KJV) God does not lead us into evil; He delivers us from it. He does not teach us to practice evil in moderation. Jesus did not make, use, approve, commend, or tell us to use intoxicating wine. The LORD God made man to have fellowship with Him and alcohol interferes with that relationship and God's purpose for mankind. Jesus said, at the last supper, "But I say unto you, I will not drink henceforth of this fruit of the vine, until that day when I drink it new with you in My Father's kingdom. (Matthew 26:29 KJV) I believe He was speaking spiritually because what does wine have to do with his "Father's kingdom."

During the Lord's Supper, Jesus made a covenant with His disciples when He said, *"For this is My blood of the new testament, which is shed for many for the remission of sins. But I say unto you, I will not drink henceforth of this fruit of the vine, until that day when I drink it new with you in My Father's kingdom."* (Matthew 26:28-29 KJV) I do not dispute there was *fruit of the vine* because our Lord said what was contained in the cup. However, everything the Christ said or did always had a deeper spiritual meaning. He used metaphors to help us understand the deeper meaning. For example, when Jesus said to them, *"....I am the bread of life; he who comes to Me will not hunger, and he who believes in Me will never thirst."* (John 6:35 KJV) Jesus compares Himself to bread as a metaphor. Because bread sustains us in life, *the bread of life*, is symbolic of eternal fulfillment. I believe Jesus is saying He can sustain His followers in a spiritual sense or He wants to continually fill us with His Spirit. . There are two verses from the Old Testament referring to the *fruit of the vine* looking like blood, Genesis 49:11 *"Binding his donkey to the vine, And his donkey's colt to the choice vine, He washed his garments in wine, And his clothes in the blood of grapes,"* and Deuteronomy 32:14 *"...And you drank wine, the blood of the grapes."* In this instance, Jesus used grapes that looked like blood, which was commonly known in His day, as a metaphor to proclaim His death. Jesus chose the *fruit of the vine* to represent His shed blood and made the connection between the blood of the grape and the blood that He soon would be shedding. Many years later after the Lord's Supper,

Christian began to memorialize the *Lord's Supper* into a ritual called Communion, also known as the Eucharist by Catholics.

Here are some additional verses giving warning against intoxicating wine. These are located in 75 different areas of the Bible speaking on the effects of alcohol:

Genesis 9:20-26 - Noah and his Descendents, Drunkenness Lead to Immorality

1) Genesis 9:20-26 –Noah's drunkenness lead to immorality and family trouble.

Genesis 9:21 And he drank of the wine, and was drunken; and he was uncovered within his tent.

Genesis 9:22 And Ham, the father of Canaan, saw the nakedness of his father, and told his two brethren without.

Genesis 9:23 And Shem and Japheth took a garment, and laid it upon both their shoulders, and went backward, and covered the nakedness of their father; and their faces were backward, and they saw not their father's nakedness.

Genesis 9:24 And Noah awoke from his wine, and knew what his younger son had done unto him.

Genesis 9:25 And he said, Cursed be Canaan; a servant of servants shall he be unto his brethren.

Genesis 9:26 And he said, Blessed be the LORD God of Shem; and Canaan shall be his servant.

Genesis 19:30-38 - Lot and His Descendants, Lot's drunkenness also led to immorality.

2) Genesis 19:30 And Lot went up out of Zoar, and dwelt in the mountain, and his two daughters with him; for he feared to dwell in Zoar: and he dwelt in a cave, he and his two daughters.

Genesis 19:31 And the firstborn said unto the younger, Our father is old, and there is not a man in the earth to come in unto us after the manner of all the earth:

Genesis 19:32 Come, let us make our father drink wine, and we will lie with him, that we may preserve seed of our father.

Genesis 19:33 And they made their father drink wine that night: and the firstborn went in, and lay with her father; and he perceived not when she lay down, nor when she arose.

Genesis 19:34 And it came to pass on the morrow, that the firstborn said unto the younger, Behold, I lay yester night with My father: let us make him drink wine this night also; and go thou in, and lie with him, that we may preserve seed of our father.

Genesis 19:35 And they made their father drink wine that night also: and the younger arose, and lay with him; and he perceived not when she lay down, nor when she arose.

Genesis 19:36 Thus were both the daughters of Lot with child by their father.

Genesis 19:37 And the firstborn bare a son, and called his name Moab: the same is the father of the Moabites unto this day.

Genesis 19:38 And the younger, she also bare a son, and called his name Benammi: the same is the father of the children of Ammon unto this day.

Leviticus 10:9-11 – The priests were order by God not to drink wine or strong drink so that they know the difference between what is holy and the unholy.

3) Leviticus 10:9 Do not drink wine nor strong drink, thou, nor thy sons with thee, when ye go into the tabernacle of the congregation, lest ye die: it shall be a statute for ever throughout your generations:

Leviticus 10:10 And that ye may put difference between holy and unholy, and between unclean and clean;

Leviticus 10:11 And that ye may teach the children of Israel all the statutes which the LORD hath spoken unto them by the hand of Moses.

Numbers 6:3 – The Nazarites were forbidden to eat or drink anything from the grape vine not even vinegar.

4) Numbers 6:1 And the LORD spake unto Moses, saying,

Numbers 6:2 All the days of his separation shall he eat nothing that is made of the vine tree, from the kernels even to the husk.

Numbers 6:3 He shall separate himself from wine and strong drink, and shall drink no vinegar of wine, or vinegar of strong drink, neither shall he drink any liquor of grapes, nor eat moist grapes, or dried.

5) Deuteronomy 21:20 – A drunken son was stubborn and rebellious.

Deuteronomy 21:20 And they shall say unto the elders of his city, This our son is stubborn and rebellious, he will not obey our voice; he is a glutton, and a drunkard.

6) Deuteronomy 29:5-6 – God gave no wine to Israel nor did they have wine or strong drink in the wilderness.

Deuteronomy 29:5 And I have led you forty years in the wilderness: your clothes are not waxen old upon you, and thy shoe is not waxen old upon thy foot.

Deuteronomy 29:6 Ye have not eaten bread, neither have ye drunk wine or strong drink: that ye might know that I am the LORD your God.

Deuteronomy 32:33 – Strong wine is like the poison of serpents and the cruel venom of asps.

7) Deuteronomy 32:33 Their wine is the poison of dragons, and the cruel venom of asps.

Judges 13:4, 7, 14 – Samson was to be a Nazarite of God for life so his mother was told not to eat or drink anything of the vine or wine or strong drink from conception.

8) Judges 13:4 Now therefore beware, I pray thee, and drink not wine nor strong drink, and eat not any unclean thing:

Judges 13:7 But he said unto me, Behold, thou shalt conceive, and bear a son; and now drink no wine nor strong drink, neither eat any unclean thing: for the child shall be a Nazarite to God from the womb to the day of his death.

Judges 13:14 She may not eat of any thing that cometh of the vine, neither let her drink wine or strong drink, nor eat any unclean thing: all that I commanded her let her observe.

1 Samuel 1:14-15 – Hannah was accused of being drunk however she said she drank no wine.

9) 1 Samuel 1:14 And Eli said unto her, How long wilt thou be drunken? put away thy wine from thee.

1 Samuel 1:15 And Hannah answered and said, No, my lord, I am a woman of a sorrowful spirit: I have drunk neither wine nor strong drink, but have poured out my soul before the LORD.

1 Samuel 25:32-38 – Nabal died after drinking all night.

10) 1 Samuel 25:32 And David said to Abigail, Blessed be the LORD God of Israel, which sent thee this day to meet me:

1 Samuel 25:33 And blessed be thy advice, and blessed be thou, which hast kept me this day from coming to shed blood, and from avenging myself with mine own hand.

1 Samuel 25:34 For in very deed, as the LORD God of Israel liveth, which hath kept me back from hurting thee, except thou hadst hasted and come to meet me, surely there had not been left unto Nabal by the morning light any that pisseth against the wall.

1 Samuel 25:35 So David received of her hand that which she had brought him, and said unto her, Go up in peace to thine house; see, I have hearkened to thy voice, and have accepted thy person.

1 Samuel 25:36 And Abigail came to Nabal; and, behold, he held a feast in his house, like the feast of a king; and Nabal's heart was merry within him, for he was very drunken: wherefore she told him nothing, less or more, until the morning light.

1 Samuel 25:37 But it came to pass in the morning, when the wine was gone out of Nabal, and his wife had told him these things, that his heart died within him, and he became as a stone.

1 Samuel 25:38 And it came to pass about ten days after, that the LORD smote Nabal, that he died.

2 Samuel 11:13 – David thought he cover his sin by getting Uriah drunk

11) 2 Samuel 11:13 And when David had called him, he did eat and drink before him; and he made him drunk: and at even he went out to lie on his bed with the servants of his lord, but went not down to his house.

2 Samuel 13:28-29 – Amnon was drunk when he was assassinated.

12) 2 Samuel 13:28 Now Absalom had commanded his servants, saying, Mark ye now when Amnon's heart is merry with wine, and when I say unto you, Smite

Amnon; then kill him, fear not: have not I commanded you? be courageous, and be valiant.

2 Samuel 13:29 And the servants of Absalom did unto Amnon as Absalom had commanded. Then all the king's sons arose, and every man gat him up upon his mule, and fled.

1 Kings 16:8-10 – The king was assassinated while getting drunk.

13) 1 Kings 16:8 In the twenty and sixth year of Asa king of Judah began Elah the son of Baasha to reign over Israel in Tirzah, two years.

1 Kings 16:9 And his servant Zimri, captain of half his chariots, conspired against him, as he was in Tirzah, drinking himself drunk in the house of Arza steward of his house in Tirzah.

1 Kings 16:10 And Zimri went in and smote him, and killed him, in the twenty and seventh year of Asa king of Judah, and reigned in his stead.

1 Kings 20:12-21 – Ben-Hadad and 32 other kings were drinking when they were attacked and defeated by the Israelites.

14) 1 Kings 20:12 And it came to pass, when Benhadad heard this message, as he was drinking, he and the kings in the pavilions, that he said unto his servants,

Set yourselves in array. And they set themselves in array against the city.

1 Kings 20:13 And, behold, there came a prophet unto Ahab king of Israel, saying, Thus saith the LORD, Hast thou seen all this great multitude? behold, I will deliver it into thine hand this day; and thou shalt know that I am the LORD.

1 Kings 20:14 And Ahab said, By whom? And he said, Thus saith the LORD, Even by the young men of the princes of the provinces. Then he said, Who shall order the battle? And he answered, Thou.

1 Kings 20:15 Then he numbered the young men of the princes of the provinces, and they were two hundred and thirty two: and after them he numbered all the people, even all the children of Israel, being seven thousand.

1 Kings 20:16 And they went out at noon. But Benhadad was drinking himself drunk in the pavilions, he and the kings, the thirty and two kings that helped him.

1 Kings 20:17 And the young men of the princes of the provinces went out first; and Benhadad sent out, and they told him, saying, There are men come out of Samaria.

1 Kings 20:18 And he said, Whether they be come out for peace, take them alive; or whether they be come out for war, take them alive.

1 Kings 20:19 So these young men of the princes of the provinces came out of the city, and the army which followed them.

1 Kings 20:20 And they slew every one his man: and the Syrians fled; and Israel pursued them: and Benhadad the king of Syria escaped on an horse with the horsemen.

1 Kings 20:21 And the king of Israel went out, and smote the horses and chariots, and slew the Syrians with a great slaughter.

Esther 1:5-12 – After the king gave everyone all the drink they wanted and he was drunk, he commanded the queen to come.

15) Esther 1:5 And when these days were expired, the king made a feast unto all the people that were present in Shushan the palace, both unto great and small, seven days, in the court of the garden of the king's palace;

Esther 1:6 Where were white, green, and blue, hangings, fastened with cords of fine linen and purple to silver rings and pillars of marble: the beds were of gold and silver, upon a pavement of red, and blue, and white, and black, marble.

Esther 1:7 And they gave them drink in vessels of gold, (the vessels being diverse one from another,) and royal wine in abundance, according to the state of the king.

Esther 1:8 And the drinking was according to the law; none did compel: for so the king had appointed to all the officers of his house, that they should do according to every man's pleasure.

Esther 1:9 Also Vashti the queen made a feast for the women in the royal house which belonged to king Ahasuerus.

Esther 1:10 On the seventh day, when the heart of the king was merry with wine, he commanded Mehuman, Biztha, Harbona, Bigtha, and Abagtha, Zethar, and Carcas, the seven chamberlains that served in the presence of Ahasuerus the king,

Esther 1:11 To bring Vashti the queen before the king with the crown royal, to shew the people and the princes her beauty: for she was fair to look on.

Esther 1:12 But the queen Vashti refused to come at the king's commandment by his chamberlains: therefore was the king very wroth, and his anger burned in him.

Psalm 75:8 – The LORD's anger is described as mixed wine poured out and drunk by the wicked of the earth.

16) Psalms 75:8 For in the hand of the LORD there is a cup, and the wine is red; it is full of mixture; and he poureth out of the same: but the dregs thereof, all the wicked of the earth shall wring them out, and drink them.

Proverbs 4:17 – Strong drink is called the wine of violence.

17) Proverbs 4:17 For they eat the bread of wickedness, and drink the wine of violence.

Proverbs 20:1 – Wine is a mocker, strong drink is raging.

18) Proverbs 20:1 Wine is a mocker, strong drink is raging: and whosoever is deceived thereby is not wise.

Proverbs 23:19-20 – A wise person will not be among the drinkers of strong drink.

19) Proverbs 23:19 Hear thou, my son, and be wise, and guide thine heart in the way.

Proverbs 23:20 Be not among winebibbers; among riotous eaters of flesh:

Proverbs 23:21 – Drunkenness causes poverty.

20) Proverbs 23:21 For the drunkard and the glutton shall come to poverty: and drowsiness shall clothe a man with rags.

Proverbs 23:29-30 – Drinking wine and mix wine causes woe, sorrow, fighting, babbling, wounds without cause and red eyes.

21) Proverbs 23:29 Who hath woe? who hath sorrow? who hath contentions? who hath babbling? who hath wounds without cause? who hath redness of eyes?

Proverbs 23:30 They that tarry long at the wine; they that go to seek mixed wine.

Proverbs 23:31 – God instructs us not to look at wine.

22) Proverbs 23:31 Look not thou upon the wine when it is red, when it giveth his colour in the cup, when it moveth itself aright.

Proverbs 23:32 – Strong drink bite like a serpent, sting like an adder.

23) Proverbs 23:32 At the last it biteth like a serpent, and stingeth like an adder.

Proverbs 23:33 – Strong drink or wine causes the drinker to have perverse adulterous thoughts.

24) Proverbs 23:33 Thine eyes shall behold strange women, and thine heart shall utter perverse things.

Proverbs 23:34 – Strong drink makes the drinker do unstable things.

> 25) Proverbs 23:34 Yea, thou shalt be as he that lieth down in the midst of the sea, or as he that lieth upon the top of a mast.

Proverbs 23:35 – Strong drink or wine makes the drinker not feel pain so he does not realize it as a warning that it is also habit forming.

> 26) Proverbs 23:35 They have stricken me, shalt thou say, and I was not sick; they have beaten me, and I felt it not: when shall I awake? I will seek it yet again.

Proverb 31:4-5 – If you rule and judge like Kings, Princes, and others, you should not drink strong drink like wine or your judgment will be impaired.

> 27) Proverbs 31:4 It is not for kings, O Lemuel, it is not for kings to drink wine; nor for princes strong drink:
>
> Proverbs 31:5 Lest they drink, and forget the law, and pervert the judgment of any of the afflicted.

Proverbs 31:6-7 – Strong drink could be given to those about to perish or those in pain.

> 28) Proverbs 31:6 Give strong drink unto him that is ready to perish, and wine unto those that be of heavy hearts.

Proverbs 31:7 Let him drink, and forget his poverty, and remember his misery no more.

Ecclesiastes 2:3 – The king tried everything, including strong drink, to see if it satisfied however it did not. (Ecclesiastes 12:8)

29) Ecclesiastes 2:3 I sought in mine heart to give myself unto wine, yet acquainting mine heart with wisdom; and to lay hold on folly, till I might see what was that good for the sons of men, which they should do under the heaven all the days of their life.

Ecclesiastes 10:17 – If a leader does not drink, the land is blessed.

30) Ecclesiastes 10:17 Blessed art thou, O land, when thy king is the son of nobles, and thy princes eat in due season, for strength, and not for drunkenness!

Isaiah 5:11-12 – Woe to them who get up early to drink and stay up late at night to get drunk.

31) Isaiah 5:11 Woe unto them that rise up early in the morning, that they may follow strong drink; that continue until night, till wine inflame them!

Isaiah 5:12 And the harp, and the viol, the tabret, and pipe, and wine, are in their feasts: but they regard not the work of the LORD, neither consider the operation of his hands.

Isaiah 5:22 – Woe to mighty drinkers and mixers of strong drink.

32) Isaiah 5:22 Woe unto them that are mighty to drink wine, and men of strength to mingle strong drink:

Isaiah 19:14 – Drunken men stagger in their vomit.

33) Isaiah 19:14 The LORD hath mingled a perverse spirit in the midst thereof: and they have caused Egypt to err in every work thereof, as a drunken man staggereth in his vomit.

Isaiah 22:12-13 – The Israelites chose to drink because they were going to die the next day.

34) Isaiah 22:12 And in that day did the LORD GOD of hosts call to weeping, and to mourning, and to baldness, and to girding with sackcloth:

Isaiah 22:13 And behold joy and gladness, slaying oxen, and killing sheep, eating flesh, and drinking wine: let us eat and drink; for tomorrow we shall die.

Isaiah 24:9 – God will judge the drinkers and they cannot escape the consequences.

35) Isaiah 24:9 They shall not drink wine with a song; strong drink shall be bitter to them that drink it.

Isaiah 28:1 – Woe to the crown of pride and drunk people of Ephraim.

36) Isaiah 28:1 Woe to the crown of pride, to the drunkards of Ephraim, whose glorious beauty is a fading flower, which are on the head of the fat valleys of them that are overcome with wine!

Isaiah 28:3 – Proud drunkards shall be trodden down.

37) Isaiah 28:3 The crown of pride, the drunkards of Ephraim, shall be trodden under feet:

Isaiah 28:7 – Priests and prophets who drink beer and wine, err in vision, and stumble in judgment.

38) Isaiah 28:7 But they also have erred through wine, and through strong drink are out of the way; the priest and the prophet have erred through strong drink, they are swallowed up of wine, they are out of the way through strong drink; they err in vision, they stumble in judgment.

Isaiah 28:8 – Drinkers leave tables full with vomit and filth.

39) Isaiah 28:8 For all tables are full of vomit and filthiness, so that there is no place clean.

Isaiah 56:9-12 – Drinkers who are greedy expect tomorrow to be just like today.

40) Isaiah 56:9 All ye beasts of the field, come to devour, yea, all ye beasts in the forest.

Isaiah 56:10 His watchmen are blind: they are all ignorant, they are all dumb dogs, they cannot bark; sleeping, lying down, loving to slumber.

Isaiah 56:11 Yea, they are greedy dogs which can never have enough, and they are shepherds that cannot understand: they all look to their own way, every one for his gain, from his quarter.

Isaiah 56:12 Come ye, say they, I will fetch wine, and we will fill ourselves with strong drink; and to morrow shall be as this day, and much more abundant.

Jeremiah 35:2-14 – The Rechabites drank no wine or strong drink and were blessed.

41) Jeremiah 35:2 Go unto the house of the Rechabites, and speak unto them, and bring them into the house of the LORD, into one of the chambers, and give them wine to drink.

Jeremiah 35:3 Then I took Jaazaniah the son of Jeremiah, the son of Habaziniah, and his brethren, and all his sons, and the whole house of the Rechabites;

Jeremiah 35:4 And I brought them into the house of the LORD, into the chamber of the sons of Hanan, the son of Igdaliah, a man of God, which was by the chamber of the princes, which was above the chamber of Maaseiah the son of Shallum, the keeper of the door:

Jeremiah 35:5 And I set before the sons of the house of the Rechabites pots full of wine, and cups, and I said unto them, Drink ye wine.

Jeremiah 35:6 But they said, We will drink no wine: for Jonadab the son of Rechab our father commanded us, saying, Ye shall drink no wine, neither ye, nor your sons for ever:

Jeremiah 35:7 Neither shall ye build house, nor sow seed, nor plant vineyard, nor have any: but all your days ye shall dwell in tents; that ye may live many days in the land where ye be strangers.

Jeremiah 35:8 Thus have we obeyed the voice of Jonadab the son of Rechab our father in all that he hath charged us, to drink no wine all our days, we, our wives, our sons, nor our daughters;

Jeremiah 35:9 Nor to build houses for us to dwell in: neither have we vineyard, nor field, nor seed:

Jeremiah 35:10 But we have dwelt in tents, and have obeyed, and done according to all that Jonadab our father commanded us.

Jeremiah 35:11 But it came to pass, when Nebuchadrezzar king of Babylon came up into the land, that we said, Come, and let us go to Jerusalem for fear of the army of the Chaldeans, and for fear of the army of the Syrians: so we dwell at Jerusalem.

Jeremiah 35:12 Then came the word of the LORD unto Jeremiah, saying,

Jeremiah 35:13 Thus saith the LORD of hosts, the God of Israel; Go and tell the men of Judah and the inhabitants of Jerusalem, Will ye not receive instruction to hearken to MY words? saith the LORD.

Jeremiah 35:14 The words of Jonadab the son of Rechab, that he commanded his sons not to drink wine, are performed; for unto this day they drink none, but obey their father's commandment: notwithstanding I have spoken unto you, rising early and speaking; but ye hearkened not unto me.

Ezekiel 44:21 –God instructed the priests not to drink wine.

42) Ezekiel 44:21 Neither shall any priest drink wine, when they enter into the inner court.

Daniel 1:5-17 – Daniel and his abstaining friends refused the king's strong drink and was blessed for it.

43) Daniel 1:5 And the king appointed them a daily provision of the king's meat, and of the wine which he drank: so nourishing them three years, that at the end thereof they might stand before the king.

Daniel 1:6 Now among these were of the children of Judah, Daniel, Hananiah, Mishael, and Azariah:

Daniel 1:7 Unto whom the prince of the eunuchs gave names: for he gave unto Daniel the name of Belteshazzar; and to Hananiah, of Shadrach; and to Mishael, of Meshach; and to Azariah, of Abednego.

Daniel 1:8 But Daniel purposed in his heart that he would not defile himself with the portion of the king's meat, nor with the wine which he drank: therefore he requested of the prince of the eunuchs that he might not defile himself.

Daniel 1:9 Now God had brought Daniel into favour and tender love with the prince of the eunuchs.

Daniel 1:10 And the prince of the eunuchs said unto Daniel, I fear my lord the king, who hath appointed your meat and your drink: for why should he see your faces worse liking than the children which are of your sort? then shall ye make me endanger my head to the king.

Daniel 1:11 Then said Daniel to Melzar, whom the prince of the eunuchs had set over Daniel, Hananiah, Mishael, and Azariah,

Daniel 1:12 Prove thy servants, I beseech thee, ten days; and let them give us pulse to eat, and water to drink.

Daniel 1:13 Then let our countenances be looked upon before thee, and the countenance of the children that eat of the portion of the king's meat: and as thou seest, deal with thy servants.

Daniel 1:14 So he consented to them in this matter, and proved them ten days.

Daniel 1:15 And at the end of ten days their countenances appeared fairer and fatter in flesh than all the children which did eat the portion of the king's meat.

Daniel 1:16 Thus Melzar took away the portion of their meat, and the wine that they should drink; and gave them pulse.

Daniel 1:17 As for these four children, God gave them knowledge and skill in all learning and wisdom: and Daniel had understanding in all visions and dreams.

Daniel 5:1 – Belshazzar, ruler of Babylon; drank wine with his people.

44) Daniel 5:1 Belshazzar the king made a great feast to a thousand of his lords, and drank wine before the thousand.

Daniel 5:2-3 – The king, along with his nobles, wives, and concubines, drank from the goblets which had been taken from God's temple.

45) Daniel 5:2 Belshazzar, whiles he tasted the wine, commanded to bring the golden and silver vessels which his father Nebuchadnezzar had taken out of the temple which was in Jerusalem; that the king, and his princes, his wives, and his concubines, might drink therein.

Daniel 5:3 Then they brought the golden vessels that were taken out of the temple of the house of God which was at Jerusalem; and the king, and his princes, his wives, and his concubines, drank in them.

Daniel 5:4 – They drank wine and praised false gods.

46) Daniel 5:4 They drank wine, and praised the gods of gold, and of silver, of brass, of iron, of wood, and of stone.

Daniel 5:23 – God sent word to Belshazzar that punishment would be swift for the evil he had committed.

47) Daniel 5:23 But hast lifted up thyself against the LORD of heaven; and they have brought the vessels of his house before thee, and thou, and thy lords, thy wives, and thy concubines, have drunk wine in them; and thou hast praised the gods of silver, and gold, of brass, iron, wood, and stone, which see not, nor hear, nor know: and the God in whose hand thy breath is, and whose are all thy ways, hast thou not glorified:

Hosea 4:11 – Drinking wine takes away your ability to think intelligently.

48) Hosea 4:11 Whoredom and wine and new wine take away the heart.

Hosea 7:5 – God punished the princes for drinking.

49) Hosea 7:5 In the day of our king the princes have made him sick with bottles of wine; he stretched out his hand with scorners.

Joel 1:1-5 – Drunkards are awakened and cry.

50) Joel 1:1 The word of the LORD that came to Joel the son of Pethuel

Joel 1:2 Hear this, ye old men, and give ear, all ye inhabitants of the land. Hath this been in your days, or even in the days of your fathers?

Joel 1:3 Tell ye your children of it, and let your children tell their children, and their children another generation.

Joel 1:4 That which the palmerworm hath left hath the locust eaten; and that which the locust hath left hath the cankerworm eaten; and that which the cankerworm hath left hath the caterpiller eaten.

Joel 1:5 Awake, ye drunkards, and weep; and howl, all ye drinkers of wine, because of the new wine; for it is cut off from your mouth.

Joel 3:3 – They sold a girl for wine and were judged.

51) Joel 3:3 And they have cast lots for my people; and have given a boy for an harlot, and sold a girl for wine, that they might drink.

Amos 2:8 – Condemned for drinking wine.

52) Amos 2:8 And they lay themselves down upon clothes laid to pledge by every altar, and they drink the wine of the condemned in the house of their god.

Amos 2:12 – They are also condemned for forcing Nazarites to drink wine.

53) Amos 2:12 But ye gave the Nazarites wine to drink; and commanded the prophets, saying, Prophesy not.

Micah 2:11 – They are eager to follow false teachers who prophesy plenty of drinking wine and strong drink.

54) Micah 2:11 If a man walking in the spirit and falsehood do lie, saying, I will prophesy unto thee of wine and of strong drink; he shall even be the prophet of this people.

Nahum 1:10 – The drunkards of Nineveh will be destroyed.

55) Nahum 1:10 For while they be folden together as thorns, and while they are drunken as drunkards, they shall be devoured as stubble fully dry.

Habakkuk 2:5 – A man is deceived by wine.

56) Habakkuk 2:5 Yea also, because he transgresseth by wine, he is a proud man, neither keepeth at home, who enlargeth his desire as hell, and is as death, and cannot be satisfied, but gathereth unto him all nations, and heapeth unto him all people:

Habakkuk 2:15 – Woe to him that gives his neighbor drink.

57) Habakkuk 2:15 Woe unto him that giveth his neighbour drink, that puttest thy bottle to him, and

makest him drunken also, that thou mayest look on their nakedness!

Habakkuk 2:16 – Drinking leads to shame.

58) Habakkuk 2:16 Thou art filled with shame for glory: drink thou also, and let thy foreskin be uncovered: the cup of the LORD'S right hand shall be turned unto thee, and shameful spewing shall be on thy glory.

Matthew 24:48-51 – A drinking servant is unprepared for his lord's return.

59) Matthew 24:48 But and if that evil servant shall say in his heart, My lord delayeth his coming;

Matthew 24:49 And shall begin to smite his fellow servants, and to eat and drink with the drunken;

Matthew 24:50 The lord of that servant shall come in a day when he looketh not for him, and in an hour that he is not aware of,

Matthew 24:51 And shall cut him asunder, and appoint him his portion with the hypocrites: there shall be weeping and gnashing of teeth.

Luke 1:15 – John the Baptist drank neither wine nor strong drink.

60) Luke 1:15 For he shall be great in the sight of the Lord, and shall drink neither wine nor strong drink;

and he shall be filled with the Holy Ghost, even from his mother's womb.

Luke 12:45 – A warning against drunkenness.

61) Luke 12:45 But and if that servant say in his heart, My lord delayeth his coming; and shall begin to beat the men servants and maidens, and to eat and drink, and to be drunken;

Luke 21:34 – Drunkenness will cause a person to be unaware of the Lord's return.

62) Luke 21:34 And take heed to yourselves, lest at any time your hearts be overcharged with surfeiting, and drunkenness, and cares of this life, and so that day come upon you unawares.

Romans 13:13 – Walk in honesty not drunkenness or immoral acts.

63) Romans 13:13 Let us walk honestly, as in the day; not in rioting and drunkenness, not in chambering and wantonness, not in strife and envying.

Romans 14:21 – Do not do anything that will cause a believer to stumble or made weak.

64) Romans 14:21 It is good neither to eat flesh, nor to drink wine, nor any thing whereby thy brother stumbleth, or is offended, or is made weak.

1 Corinthians 5:11 – Do not associate with a brother who drink and commit immoral acts.

65) 1 Corinthians 5:11 But now I have written unto you not to keep company, if any man that is called a brother be a fornicator, or covetous, or an idolater, or a railer, or a drunkard, or an extortioner; with such a one no not to eat.

1 Corinthians 6:10 – Drunkards will not inherit the kingdom of God

66) 1 Corinthians 6:10 Nor thieves, nor covetous, nor drunkards, nor revilers, nor extortioners, shall inherit the kingdom of God.

Galatians 5:21 – A person who commit immoral and sinful acts, such as envy and drunkenness, will not inherit the kingdom of God.

67) Galatians 5:21 Envyings, murders, drunkenness, revellings, and such like: of which I tell you before, as I have also told you in time past, that they which do such things shall not inherit the kingdom of God.

Ephesians 5:18 – Rather than be drunk with wine, a believer should be filled with the Spirit.

68) Ephesians 5:18 And be not drunk with wine, wherein is excess; but be filled with the Spirit;

1 Thessalonians 5:6-7 – Christians are to be watchful and sober rather than drunkards of the night.

69) 1 Thessalonians 5:6 Therefore let us not sleep, as do others; but let us watch and be sober.

1 Thessalonians 5:7 For they that sleep, sleep in the night; and they that be drunken are drunken in the night.

1 Timothy 3:2-3 – Bishops must be of good moral character and not give in to wine which brings bad behavior.

70) 1 Timothy 3:1 This is a true saying, if a man desire the office of a bishop, he desireth a good work.

1 Timothy 3:2 A bishop then must be blameless, the husband of one wife, vigilant, sober, of good behavior, given to hospitality, apt to teach;

1 Timothy 3:3 Not given to wine, no striker, not greedy of filthy lucre; but patient, not a brawler, not covetous;

1 Timothy 3:4 One that ruleth well his own house, having his children in subjection with all gravity;

1 Timothy 3:5 (For if a man know not how to rule his own house, how shall he take care of the church of God?)

1 Timothy 3:8 – Deacons must also be of good moral character and not drinkers.

> 71) 1 Timothy 3:8 Likewise must the deacons be grave, not double tongued, not given to much wine, not greedy of filthy lucre;

1 Timothy 3:11 – Deacons' wives also must be of good moral character and sober.

> 72) 1 Timothy 3:11 Even so must their wives be grave, not slanderers, sober, faithful in all things.

Titus 1:7-8 – The stewards of God must be holy, disciplined, temperate and sober.

> 73) Titus 1:7 For a bishop must be blameless, as the steward of God; not self willed, not soon angry, not given to wine, no striker, not given to filthy lucre;

> Titus 1:8 But a lover of hospitality, a lover of good men, sober, just, holy, temperate;

Titus 2:2-3 – The elders or older men and older women of the church must exemplify holiness and also be disciplined, temperate and sober.

> 74) Titus 2:2 That the aged men be sober, grave, temperate, sound in faith, in charity, in patience.

Titus 2:3 The aged women likewise, that they be in behaviour as becometh holiness, not false accusers, not given to much wine, teachers of good things;

1 Peter 4:3-4 – If a member of the church has repented and is born again then the past life of drunkenness and carousing has no place in the Christian's life.

75) 1 Peter 4:3 For the time past of our life may suffice us to have wrought the will of the Gentiles, when we walked in lasciviousness, lusts, excess of wine, revellings, banquetings, and abominable idolatries:

1 Peter 4:4 Wherein they think it strange that ye run not with them to the same excess of riot, speaking evil of you.

Proverbs 23:20-21

Proverb 23:20 Be not among winebibbers; among riotous eaters of flesh:

Proverbs 23:21 For the drunkard and the glutton shall come to poverty: and drowsiness shall clothe a man with rags.

Proverbs 23:29-33-The Bible gives a perfect description of the effects of alcohol in.

Proverb 23:29 Who hath woe? who hath sorrow? who hath contentions? who hath babbling? who hath wounds without cause? who hath redness of eyes?

Proverb 23:30 They that tarry long at the wine; they that go to seek mixed wine.

Proverb 23:31 Look not thou upon the wine when it is red, when it giveth his colour in the cup, when it moveth itself aright.

Proverb 23:32 At the last it biteth like a serpent, and stingeth like an adder. 33 Thine eyes shall behold strange women, and thine heart shall utter perverse things.

The Miracles of Jesus - In Biblical Order

There were many miracles of God in the Old Testament, such as the ten plagues of Egypt, the parting of the Red Sea, the manna from heaven, the water from a rock and Daniel in the lion's den, and many others. However, the miracles which Jesus performed were distinctive. These miracles were considered signs and mighty work which confirmed His divinity and His mission. While many were already familiar with miracles of the LORD God, however, the following response to Jesus miracles were unique and they said, "...*they were all amazed, and glorified God, saying, We never saw it on this fashion. And they were astonished with a great astonishment. ...and they were sore amazed in themselves beyond measure, and wondered. And were beyond measure astonished, saying, He hath done all things well.*" (Mark 2:12, 5:42, 6:51, 7:37 KJV) What Jesus did was special because, "*God anointed Jesus of Nazareth with the Holy Spirit and with power, who went about doing good and healing all who were oppressed by the devil, for God was with Him.*" (Acts 10:38)

Everywhere Jesus went something special occurred that affected the people in a positive way. The following is a list of the miracles of Jesus in Biblical in the order according to scripture: "*And truly Jesus did many other signs in the presence of His disciples, which are not written in this book; but these are written that you may believe that Jesus is the Christ, the Son of God, and that believing you may have life in His name.*" (John 20:30, 31) *And Jesus went about all Galilee, teaching in their synagogues, and preaching the gospel of the kingdom, and healing all manner of sickness and all manner of disease among the people. (Matthew 4:23)*

Control of Nature

1. Calming the storm – He calmed the sea. Matthew 8:23-27; Mark 4:37-41; Luke 8:22-25

2. Feeding 5,000 – He fed 5,000 with just a few fish and bread. Matthew 14:14-21; Mark 6:30-44; Luke 9:10-17; John 6:1-14

3. Walking on water – He walked on water. Matthew 14:22-32; Mark 6:47-52; John 6:16-21

4. Feeding 4,000 – He fed 4,000. Matthew 15:32-39; Mark 8:1-9

5. Fish with coin – Jesus told Peter to catch a fish and he would find a coin in its mouth to pay a collector. Matthew 17:24-27

6. Fig tree withers – Matthew 21:18-22; Mark 11:12-14, 20-25

7. Huge catch of fish – Luke 5:4-11; John 21:1-11

8. **<u>Water into wine – John 2:1-11</u>** (See Chapter 1 & 2 of this book)

Healing of Individuals

1. Man with leprosy-healed – Matthew 8:1-4; Mark 1:40-44; Luke 5:12-14

2. Roman centurion's servant-cured – Matthew 8:5-13; Luke 7:1- 10

3. Peter's mother-in-law-fever cured – Matthew 8:14-15; Mark 1:30-31; Luke 4:38-39

4. Two men possessed with devils – Cast out into pigs who jumped off a cliff. Matthew 8:28-34; Mark 5:1- 15; Luke 8:27-39

5. Man with palsy –cured Matthew 9:2-7; Mark 2:3-12; Luke 5:18- 26

6. Woman with bleeding-cured by touching His hem – Matthew 9:20-22; Mark 5:25-34; Luke 8:43-48

7. Two blind men –sight returned Matthew 9:27-31

8. Dumb, devil-possessed man-Dumb spoke and devil casted out - Matthew 9:32-33

9. Canaanite woman's daughter-healed – Matthew 15:21-28; Mark 7:24-30

10. Boy with devil-devil casted out - Matthew 17:14-21; Mark 9:17-29; Luke 9:38- 43

11. Two blind men-sight restored – including Bartimaeus - Matthew 20:29-34; Mark 10:46-52; Luke 18:35-43

12. Demon-possessed man in synagogue-demon casted out – Mark 1:21-28; Luke 4:31-37

13. Blind man at Bethsaida-sight restored – Mark 8:22-26

14. Crippled woman-made to walk – Luke 13:10-17

15. Man with dropsy-cured – Luke 14:1-4

16. Ten men with leprosy-cured – Luke 17:11-19

17. The high priest's servant –Healed a man's cut off ear Luke 22:50-51

18. Nobleman's son at Capernaum-cured – John 4:46-54

19. Sick man at the pool of Bethsaida-cured – John 5:1-15

20. Man born blind-sight restored – John 9:1-41

Raising the Dead

1. Jairus' daughter-brought back to life – Matthew 9:18-26; Mark 5:21-43; Luke 8:40-56

2. Widow's son at Nain-restored to life – Luke 7:11-17

3. Lazarus-brought back alive – John 11:1-44

As you can see above, under "Control of Nature, number 8, water into wine is listed as a miracle according to some, however, I have proven through scripture, that only "the servants which drew the water knew:" and that the governor who "knew not whence it was (John 2:9)," said it was wine. If you compare that to all the other miracles performed by Jesus and in view of all the other scriptures stated in the Bible about the negative effects of drinking alcohol on people, you should conclude that water was not turned into wine. Also, in Proverbs 23:32, the Bible compares alcohol to a serpent's bite, ". . . at last it biteth like a serpent." A serpent's bite is a deadly poison and therefore alcohol is a deadly poison.

Medical Affect of Alcohol

Alcohol poisons every major organ in your body and according to *The Birmingham News* (Nov. 19, 1990), "Scientific data show alcohol is the most physically deteriorating drug there is. It causes more organic damage than any other drug. . ." The reason people tend to throw up when drunk is because the stomach knows poison when it is coming down. It is no joke when a bartender says, "Name your poison!" When someone is drunk, they are intoxicated. Toxic is another word for poison. A drunken person has poisoned themselves with alcohol.

Although statistics show alcohol as the third cause of death, it is probably number one, because if someone has been drinking for 25 or 30 years and has a heart attack, then the death is due to drinking not heart failure.

A Few Alcohol (Ethanol) Addiction Statistics and Facts

"The adverse effects of alcohol abuse are devastating on a personal level and on a societal level," says Gregg Homanics, a professor of anesthesiology and pharmacology & chemical biology at the University of Pittsburgh. He also states that, "Alcohol abuse costs our society more than the costs of all illegal drug abuse combined." It is well documented the alcohol (ethanol) effects on the whole body, however, the brain is the primary target.

How Alcohol Affects the Brain According to Office of the Surgeon General

Alcohol affects an adolescent's brain development in many ways. The effects of underage drinking on specific brain activities are explained below. Alcohol is a central nervous system depressant. Alcohol can appear to be a stimulant because, initially, it depresses the part of the brain that controls inhibitions.

CEREBRAL CORTEX— In this part of the brain, where thoughts are processes through our senses alcohol slows things down.

CENTRAL NERVOUS SYSTEM—When a person thinks of something he wants his body to do, the central nervous system—the brain and the spinal cord—sends a signal to that part of the body. Alcohol slows down the central nervous system, making the person think, speak, and move slower.

FRONTAL LOBES—The brain's frontal lobes are important for planning, forming ideas, making decisions, and using self-control. When alcohol affects the frontal lobes of the brain, a person may find it hard to control his or her emotions and urges. The person may act without thinking or may even become violent.

Drinking alcohol over a long period of time can damage the frontal lobes forever.

HIPPOCAMPUS—The hippocampus is the part of the brain where memories are made. When alcohol reaches the hippocampus, a person may have trouble remembering something he or she just learned, such as a name or a phone number. This can happen after just one or two drinks.

Drinking a lot of alcohol quickly can cause a blackout—not being able to remember entire events, such as what he or she did last night.

If alcohol damages the hippocampus, a person may find it hard to learn and to hold on to knowledge.

CEREBELLUM—The cerebellum is important for coordination, thoughts, and awareness. A person may have trouble with these skills when alcohol enters the cerebellum. After drinking alcohol, a person's hands may be so shaky that they can't touch or grab things normally, and they may lose their balance and fall.

HYPOTHALAMUS—The hypothalamus is a small part of the brain that does an amazing number of the body's housekeeping chores. Alcohol upsets the work of the hypothalamus. After a person drinks alcohol, blood pressure, hunger, thirst, and the urge to urinate increase while body temperature and heart rate decrease.

MEDULLA—The medulla controls the body's automatic actions, such as a person's heartbeat. It also keeps the body at the right temperature. Alcohol actually chills the body. Drinking a lot of alcohol outdoors in cold weather can cause a person's body temperature to fall below normal. This dangerous condition is called hypothermia.

The term "sluding" is used to describe the effect alcohol which causes coagulation of the red corpuscles making it thick which clogs the blood stream decreasing the exchange of oxygen. Sluding is occurring when there is slurred speech and stumbling of a drunken person. Alcohol deprives the brain of life giving oxygen and brain cells die. These brain cells are the only cells that **do not reproduce** and **can never be replaced**. Autopsies on heavy drinkers reveal hollow cavities in the skull where entire areas of the brain have disappeared. And according to studies by Dr. Melvin H. Kinsley, **brain damage occurs progressively from the very first drink.** The next time you see that man staggering drunk - you are watching a man literally destroying his brain. Here are more facts:

75,000 deaths are attributable to alcohol consumption each year

Economic costs associated with alcohol problems total more than $184 billion annually

One-third of Americans report that alcohol has caused problems in their immediate family

Alcohol is the number one drug in America

The younger you start the easier it is to become addicted

It is easy and cheap to purchase and attracts youth with its sweet taste like a soft drink

Alcoholism breaks up homes and destroys communities

Many crimes are committed while under the influence of alcohol

Drinking alcohol while driving account for many accidents on the highway

Alcohol is usually involved when there is violence and abuse against women and children

There are over 18 million alcoholics in America

Cirrhosis of the liver kills over 30,000 each year and rising

50 percent of the people on welfare are due to alcohol abuse

80 percent of all fire deaths are due to alcohol abuse

65 percent of the drowning

22 percent of home accidents

77 percent of falls

36 percent of pedestrian accidents

65 percent of all murders

40 percent of all assaults

35 percent of all rapes

30 percent of other sex crimes

30 percent of all suicides

Over 80 percent of all arrests are linked to alcohol!

60 percent of all child abuse is attributed to alcohol

If we can wage a war on crack, on cocaine, on heroin, and marijuana, why can't we also wage a war on alcohol? Recently, a judge found two Steubenville, Ohio teenagers guilty of raping a 16-year-old girl "in a case that showcased jaw-dropping examples of teenage alcohol use and tawdry text messaging," according to Michael Pearson, CNN. Another example teenage alcohol use related incident occurred on March 18, 2013, when a confused 16 year old teenager who had been drinking with friends was shot and killed after he mistakenly entered a neighbor's house [which was two doors down from his own home] through a back window. In these two instances, three lives were ruined and one life tragically ended due to alcohol use.

Happy Hour is not happy when drunk drivers drive and end up killing, murdering, and maiming people due to the intoxicating effects of alcohol. Drunk people are turning our highways into demolition derby and rivers of blood. Every 12 minutes an innocent victim is killed by a drunk driver and almost 700 a week will be killed, 100 a day, nearly 5 an hour.

Over 25 million Americans have died in traffic accidents because of alcohol.

The Bible says, "Wine is a mocker, strong drink is raging: and whosoever is deceived thereby is not wise." Prov. 20:1 The Bible also teaches, "Be sober, be vigilant; because your adversary the devil, as a roaring lion, walketh about, seeking whom he may devour." 1Peter 5:8

Chapter III

"Scriptures To Live By"

"But of that day and hour knoweth no man, no, not the angels of heaven, but My Father only." Matthew 24:36

"Watch therefore, for ye know neither the day nor the hour wherein the Son of man cometh." Matthew 25:13

The parable of the fig tree tells us that we may get certain signs which show the season of Jesus return, such as, summer is coming soon because the fig tree is sprouting new leaves. However, Jesus said we still may not know until certain things come to pass within a generation and we are not meant to know the day or hour of His coming. Noah, who was considered godly among his generation, spent years building the Ark and he may have known the season, however, he did not know the day or hour the flood would come until God shut the doors. The Bible also says, in Noah's days, people were going about their day doing regular things such as eating, drinking, marrying, etc., and then the flood took them away.

Similarly, when Jesus returns people will be going about their day and like it says in Matthew 24:40, "Then there will be two men in the field; one will be taken and one left. In the parable about the ten virgins, five virgins had oil for their lamps and five did not have oil and just like us when the engine light in your car is warning us that we are about to run out of gas, we should not ignore it and get a fill to prepare for the next day. Well, when Jesus returned, the five virgins who had oil were prepared and went in with Him to the marriage (Matthew 25:1-13 KJV) and those who were not prepared just like with Noah, the door was shut and Jesus knew not the other five unprepared virgins.

The Parable of the Ten Virgins, Matthew 25:1-13 KJV

> 1 At that time the kingdom of heaven will be like ten virgins who took their lamps and went out to meet the bridegroom.
>
> 2 Five of them were foolish and five were wise.
>
> 3 The foolish ones took their lamps but did not take any oil with them.
>
> 4 The wise ones, however, took oil in jars along with their lamps.
>
> 5 The bridegroom was a long time in coming, and they all became drowsy and fell asleep.

6 At midnight the cry rang out: 'Here's the bridegroom! Come out to meet him!

7 Then all the virgins woke up and trimmed their lamps.

8 The foolish ones said to the wise, 'Give us some of your oil; our lamps are going out.'

9 No,' they replied, 'there may not be enough for both us and you. Instead, go to those who sell oil and buy some for yourselves.'

10 But while they were on their way to buy the oil, the bridegroom arrived. The virgins who were ready went in with him to the wedding banquet. And the door was shut.

11 Later the others also came. 'Lord, Lord,' they said, 'open the door for us!'

12 But he replied, 'Truly I tell you, I don't know you.'

13 Therefore keep watch, because you do not know the day or the hour.

In conclusion, in Matthew 24:44, it says "Therefore you also must be ready, because the Son of Man will come at an hour when you do not expect him."

Mark 8:11-38 King James Version (KJV)
The Feeding of 5000

11 And the Pharisees came forth, and began to question with Him, seeking of him a sign from heaven, tempting him.

12 And He sighed deeply in his spirit, and saith, Why doth this generation seek after a sign? verily I say unto you, There shall no sign be given unto this generation.

13 And He left them, and entering into the ship again departed to the other side.

14 Now the disciples had forgotten to take bread, neither had they in the ship with them more than one loaf.

15 And He charged them, saying, Take heed, beware of the leaven of the Pharisees, and of the leaven of Herod.

16 And they reasoned among themselves, saying, It is because we have no bread.

17 And when Jesus knew it, He saith unto them, Why reason ye, because ye have no bread? perceive ye not yet, neither understand? have ye your heart yet hardened?

18 Having eyes, see ye not? and having ears, hear ye not? and do ye not remember?

19 When I brake the five loaves among five thousand, how many baskets full of fragments took ye up? They say unto him, Twelve.

20 And when the seven among four thousand, how many baskets full of fragments took ye up? And they said, Seven.

21 And He said unto them, How is it that ye do not understand?

22 And He cometh to Bethsaida; and they bring a blind man unto him, and besought him to touch him.

23 And He took the blind man by the hand, and led him out of the town; and when He had spit on his eyes, and put his hands upon him, He asked him if he saw ought.

24 And he looked up, and said, I see men as trees, walking.

25 After that He put his hands again upon his eyes, and made him look up: and he was restored, and saw every man clearly.

26 And He sent him away to his house, saying, Neither go into the town, nor tell it to any in the town.

27 And Jesus went out, and his disciples, into the towns of Caesarea Philippi: and by the way He asked his disciples, saying unto them, Whom do men say that I am?

28 And they answered, John the Baptist; but some say, Elias; and others, One of the prophets.

29 And He saith unto them, But whom say ye that I am? And Peter answereth and saith unto him, Thou art the Christ.

30 And He charged them that they should tell no man of him.

31 And He began to teach them, that the Son of man must suffer many things, and be rejected of the elders, and of the chief priests, and scribes, and be killed, and after three days rise again.

32 And He spake that saying openly. And Peter took him, and began to rebuke him.

33 But when He had turned about and looked on his disciples, He rebuked Peter, saying, Get thee behind me, Satan: for thou savourest not the things that be of God, but the things that be of men.

34 And when He had called the people unto him with his disciples also, He said unto them, Whosoever will

come after me, let him deny himself, and take up his cross, and follow me.

35 For whosoever will save his life shall lose it; but whosoever shall lose his life for My sake and the gospel's, the same shall save it.

36 For what shall it profit a man, if he shall gain the whole world, and lose his own soul?

37 Or what shall a man give in exchange for his soul?

38 Whosoever therefore shall be ashamed of Me and of My words in this adulterous and sinful generation; of him also shall the Son of man be ashamed, when He cometh in the glory of His Father with the holy angels.

The Parable of the Fig Tree, Matthew 24:32-44 King James Version (KJV)

32 Learn this parable from the fig tree: Whenever its branch becomes tender and puts out its leaves, you know that summer is near.

33 So also you, when you see all these things, know that He is near, right at the door.

34 I tell you the truth, this generation will not pass away until all these things take place.

35 Heaven and earth will pass away, but MY words will never pass away.

36 But as for that day and hour no one knows it not even the angels in heaven except the Father alone.

37 For just like the days of Noah were, so the coming of the Son of Man will be.

38 For in those days before the flood, people were eating and drinking, marrying and giving in marriage, until the day Noah entered the ark.

39 And they knew nothing until the flood came and took them all away. It will be the same at the coming of the Son of Man.

40 Then there will be two men in the field; one will be taken and one left.

41 There will be two women grinding grain with a mill; one will be taken and one left.

42 Therefore stay alert, because you do not know on what day your Lord will come.

43 But understand this: If the owner of the house had known at what time of night the thief was coming, he would have been alert and would not have let his house be broken into.

44 Therefore you also must be ready, because the Son of Man will come at an hour when you do not expect him

Luke 19:1-10 King James Version (KJV)
Zacchaeus and the Sycomore Tree

19:1 And Jesus entered and passed through Jericho.

2 And, behold, there was a man named Zacchaeus, which was the chief among the publicans, and he was rich.

3 And he sought to see Jesus who He was; and could not for the press, because he was little of stature.

4 And he ran before, and climbed up into a sycomore tree to see him: for he was to pass that way.

5 And when Jesus came to the place, He looked up, and saw him, and said unto him, Zacchaeus, make haste, and come down; for to day I must abide at thy house.

6 And he made haste, and came down, and received him joyfully.

7 And when they saw it, they all murmured, saying, That He was gone to be guest with a man that is a sinner.

8 And Zacchaeus stood, and said unto the Lord: Behold, Lord, the half of my goods I give to the poor; and if I have taken any thing from any man by false accusation, I restore him fourfold.

9 And Jesus said unto him, This day is salvation come to this house, forsomuch as He also is a son of Abraham.

10 For the Son of man is come to seek and to save that which was lost.

What the Bible Say About Fruit
Psalm 127:3 King James Version (KJV)

3 Lo, children are an heritage of the LORD: and the fruit of the womb is his reward.

Matthew 7:16 King James Version (KJV)

16 Ye shall know them by their fruits. Do men gather grapes of thorns, or figs of thistles?

Matthew 13:23 King James Version (KJV)

23 But he that received seed into the good ground is he that heareth the word, and understandeth it; which also beareth fruit, and bringeth forth, some an hundredfold, some sixty, some thirty.

Mark 4:28 King James Version (KJV)

28 For the earth bringeth forth fruit of herself; first the blade, then the ear, after that the full corn in the ear.

John 12:24 King James Version (KJV)

24 Verily, verily, I say unto you, Except a corn of wheat fall into the ground and die, it abideth alone: but if it die, it bringeth forth much fruit.

John 15:2 King James Version (KJV)

2 Every branch in me that beareth not fruit He taketh away: and every branch that beareth fruit, He purgeth it, that it may bring forth more fruit.

Galatians 5:22- James Version (KJV)

22 But the fruit of the Spirit is love, joy, peace, longsuffering, gentleness, goodness, faith,

23 Meekness, temperance: against such there is no law.

More Good Scriptures to Live By

A good name is rather to be chosen than great riches, and loving favor rather than silver and gold. Proverbs 22:1. In addition to a good name is having character and one of the things that build a good character is having integrity. What does the Bible have to say about integrity?

Integrity means treating people fairly and honestly. (Leviticus 19:35-36, Deut 25:15, Proverbs 16:11-13)

Leviticus 19:35 Ye shall do no unrighteousness in judgment, in meteyard, in weight, or in measure.

Leviticus 19:36 Just balances, just weights, a just ephah, and a just hin, shall ye have: I am the LORD your God, which brought you out of the land of Egypt.

Deuteronomy 25:15 But thou shalt have a perfect and just weight, a perfect and just measure shalt thou have: that thy days may be lengthened in the land which the LORD thy God giveth thee.

Proverbs 16:11 A just weight and balance are the LORD'S: all the weights of the bag are his work.

Proverbs 16:12 It is an abomination to kings to commit wickedness: for the throne is established by righteousness.

Proverbs 16:13 Righteous lips are the delight of kings; and they love him that speaketh right.

Exodus 8:28-32 Integrity is giving your word and keeping it.

Exodus 8:28 And Pharaoh said, I will let you go, that ye may sacrifice to the LORD your God in the wilderness; only ye shall not go very far away: intreat for me.

Exodus 8:29 And Moses said, Behold, I go out from thee, and I will intreat the LORD that the swarms of flies may depart from Pharaoh, from his servants, and from his people, tomorrow: but let not Pharaoh deal deceitfully any more in not letting the people go to sacrifice to the LORD.

Exodus 8:30 And Moses went out from Pharaoh, and intreated the LORD.

Exodus 8:31 And the LORD did according to the word of Moses; and he removed the swarms of flies from Pharaoh, from his servants, and from his people; there remained not one.

Exodus 8:32 And Pharaoh hardened his heart at this time also, neither would he let the people go.

Integrity will protect you. In Psalm 25, David prays that integrity and uprightness will protect him. How can it? (Psalm 25:21, Proverbs 2:7-8, 10:9, 11:3, 13:6)

Psalms 25:21 Let integrity and uprightness preserve me; for I wait on thee.

Proverbs 2:7 He layeth up sound wisdom for the righteous: He is a buckler to them that walk uprightly.

Proverbs 2:8 He keepeth the paths of judgment, and preserveth the way of his saints.

Proverbs 10:9 He that walketh uprightly walketh surely: but he that perverteth his ways shall be known.

Proverbs 11:3 The integrity of the upright shall guide them: but the perverseness of transgressors shall destroy them.

Proverbs 13:6 Righteousness keepeth him that is upright in the way: but wickedness overthroweth the sinner.

Integrity is more valuable than riches. (Proverbs 28:6)

Proverbs 28:6 Better is the poor that walketh in his uprightness, than he that is perverse in his ways, though he be rich.

The LORD will test and judge your integrity. (1 Chronicles 29:17, Psalm 7:8)

1 Chronicles 29:17 I know also, my God, that thou triest the heart, and hast pleasure in uprightness. As for me, in the uprightness of mine heart I have willingly offered all these things: and now have I seen with joy thy people, which are present here, to offer willingly unto thee.

Psalms 7:8 The LORD shall judge the people: judge me, O LORD, according to my righteousness, and according to mine integrity that is in me.

The LORD hates lies and lack of integrity. (Zechariah 8:16-17)

Zechariah 8:16 These are the things that ye shall do; Speak ye every man the truth to his neighbour; execute the judgment of truth and peace in your gates:

Zechariah 8:17 And let none of you imagine evil in your hearts against his neighbour; and love no false oath: for all these are things that I hate, saith the LORD.

It may be difficult to maintain your integrity. (Job 2:3, 2:9, Proverbs 29:10)

Job 2:3 And the LORD said unto Satan, Hast thou considered my servant Job, that there is none like him in the earth, a perfect and an upright man, one that feareth God, and escheweth evil? and still he holdeth fast his integrity, although thou movedst me against him, to destroy him without cause.

Job 2:9 Then said his wife unto him, Dost thou still retain thine integrity? curse God, and die.

Proverbs 29:10 The bloodthirsty hate the upright: but the just seek his soul.

Your character can be corrupted by bad company. (1 Corinthians 15:33)

1 Corinthians 15:33 Be not deceived: evil communications corrupt good manners.

Integrity will be rewarded. (1 Kings 9:4-5, Nehemiah 7:2, Psalm 41:11-12)

1 Kings 9:4 And if thou wilt walk before me, as David thy father walked, in integrity of heart, and in uprightness, to do according to all that I have commanded thee, and wilt keep MY statutes and MY judgments:

1 Kings 9:5 Then I will establish the throne of thy kingdom upon Israel for ever, as I promised to David thy father, saying, There shall not fail thee a man upon the throne of Israel.

Nehemiah 7:2 That I gave my brother Hanani, and Hananiah the ruler of the palace, charge over Jerusalem: for he was a faithful man, and feared God above many.

Psalms 41:11 By this I know that thou favourest me, because mine enemy doth not triumph over me.

Psalms 41:12 And as for me, thou upholdest me in mine integrity, and settest me before thy face for ever.

Your integrity should set an example. (Titus 2:7)

Titus 2:7 In all things shewing thyself a pattern of good works: in doctrine shewing uncorruptness, gravity, sincerity......

Favorite Biblical Teachings: Verses & Parables

Proverbs 4:7 Wisdom is the principal thing; therefore get wisdom: and with all thy getting get understanding.

James 1:19 Wherefore, my beloved brethren, let every man be swift to hear, slow to speak, slow to wrath:

Proverbs 3:5 Trust in the LORD with all thine heart; and lean not unto thine own understanding.

Proverbs 3:6 In all thy ways acknowledge Him, and He shall direct thy paths.

1 Corinthians 13:2 And though I have the gift of prophecy, and understand all mysteries, and all knowledge; and though I have all faith, so that I could remove mountains, and have not charity, I am nothing. "And now abideth faith, hope, charity, these three; but the greatest of these [is] charity. 1 Corinthians 13:13.

James 1:27 Pure religion and undefiled before God and the Father is this, To visit the fatherless and widows in their affliction, and to keep himself unspotted from the world.

James 1:22 But be ye doers of the word, and not hearers only, deceiving your own selves.

Romans 15:1 We then that are strong ought to bear the infirmities of the weak, and not to please ourselves.

"If any man among you seem to be religious, and bridleth not his tongue, but deceiveth his own heart, this man's religion is vain." James 1:26

Ecclesiastes 12:1 Remember now thy Creator in the days of thy youth, while the evil days come not, nor the years draw nigh, when thou shalt say, I have no pleasure in them;

Psalms 90:4 For a thousand years in thy sight are but as yesterday when it is past, and as a watch in the night.

Psalms 90:6 In the morning it flourisheth, and groweth up; in the evening it is cut down, and withereth.

1 Corinthians 15:51 Behold, I shew you a mystery; We shall not all sleep, but we shall all be changed,

1 Corinthians 15:52 In a moment, in the twinkling of an eye, at the last trump: for the trumpet shall sound, and the dead shall be raised incorruptible, and we shall be changed.

1 Corinthians 15:53 For this corruptible must put on incorruption, and this mortal must put on immortality.

1 Corinthians 15:54 So when this corruptible shall have put on incorruption, and this mortal shall have put on immortality, then shall be brought to pass the saying that is written, Death is swallowed up in victory.

1 Corinthians 15:55 O death, where is thy sting? O grave, where is thy victory?

1 Corinthians 15:56 The sting of death is sin; and the strength of sin is the law.

1 Corinthians 15:57 But thanks be to God, which giveth us the victory through our Lord Jesus Christ.

1 Corinthians 15:58 Therefore, my beloved brethren, be ye stedfast, unmoveable, always abounding in the work of the Lord, forasmuch as ye know that your labour is not in vain in the Lord.

Matthew 7:13 Enter ye in at the strait gate: for wide is the gate, and broad is the way, that leadeth to destruction, and many there be which go in thereat:

Matthew 7:14 Because strait is the gate, and narrow is the way, which leadeth unto life, and few there be that find it.

Matthew 12:36King James Version (KJV)

36 But I say unto you, That every idle word that men shall speak, they shall give account thereof in the day of judgment.

Matthew 18:11-14King James Version (KJV)

11 For the Son of man is come to save that which was lost.

12 How think ye? if a man have an hundred sheep, and one of them be gone astray, doth He not leave the ninety and nine, and goeth into the mountains, and seeketh that which is gone astray?

13 And if so be that He find it, verily I say unto you, He rejoiceth more of that sheep, than of the ninety and nine which went not astray.

14 Even so it is not the will of your Father which is in heaven, that one of these little ones should perish.

Matthew 20: 16 So the last shall be first, and the first last: for many be called, but few chosen.

Romans 12:2 And be not conformed to this world: but be ye transformed by the renewing of your mind, that ye may prove what is that good, and acceptable, and perfect, will of God.

Philippians 2:10-11 King James Version (KJV)

10 That at the name of Jesus every knee should bow, of things in heaven, and things in earth, and things under the earth;

11 And that every tongue should confess that Jesus Christ is Lord, to the glory of God the Father.

2 Timothy 3:15 And that from a child thou hast known the Holy Scriptures, which are able to make thee wise unto salvation through faith which is in Christ Jesus.

Matthew 11:27 All things are delivered unto Me of My Father: and no man knoweth the Son, but the Father; neither knoweth any man the Father, save the Son, and he to whomsoever the Son will reveal him.

Matthew 11:28 Come unto me, all ye that labour and are heavy laden, and I will give you rest.

Matthew 11:29 TakeMy yoke upon you, and learn of me; for I am meek and lowly in heart: and ye shall find rest unto your souls.

Matthew 11:30 For My yoke is easy, andMy burden is light.

Matthew 22:37 Jesus said unto him, Thou shalt love the LORD thy God with all thy heart, and with all thy soul, and with all thy mind.

Matthew 22:38 This is the first and great commandment.

Matthew 22:39 And the second is like unto it, Thou shalt love thy neighbour as thyself.

Matthew 22:40 On these two commandments hang all the law and the prophets.

Matthew 26:26 And as they were eating, Jesus took bread, and blessed it, and brake it, and gave it to the disciples, and said, Take, eat; this is My body.

Matthew 26:27 And He took the cup, and gave thanks, and gave it to them, saying, Drink ye all of it;

Matthew 26:28 For this is My blood of the new testament, which is shed for many for the remission of sins.

Matthew 26:29 But I say unto you, I will not drink henceforth of this fruit of the vine, until that day when I drink it new with you in Father's kingdom.

Matthew 5:16 Let your light so shine before men, that they may see your good works, and glorify your Father which is in heaven.

Matthew 22:29 Jesus answered and said unto them, Ye do err, not knowing the scriptures, nor the power of God.

Luke 8:5 A sower went out to sow his seed: and as he sowed, some fell by the way side; and it was trodden down, and the fowls of the air devoured it.

Luke 8:6 And some fell upon a rock; and as soon as it was sprung up, it withered away, because it lacked moisture.

Luke 8:7 And some fell among thorns; and the thorns sprang up with it, and choked it.

Luke 8:8 And other fell on good ground, and sprang up, and bare fruit an hundredfold. And when he had said these things, he cried, He that hath ears to hear, let him hear.

Matthew 7:3 And why beholdest thou the mote that is in thy brother's eye, but considerest not the beam that is in thine own eye?

Matthew 7:4 Or how wilt thou say to thy brother, Let me pull out the mote out of thine eye; and, behold, a beam is in thine own eye?

Matthew 7:5 Thou hypocrite, first cast out the beam out of thine own eye; and then shalt thou see clearly to cast out the mote out of thy brother's eye.

James 1:19 Wherefore, my beloved brethren, let every man be swift to hear, slow to speak, slow to wrath:

Remember the Creator
Ecclesiastes 12 King James Version (KJV)

1 Remember now thy Creator in the days of thy youth, while the evil days come not, nor the years draw nigh, when thou shalt say, I have no pleasure in them;

2 While the sun, or the light, or the moon, or the stars, be not darkened, nor the clouds return after the rain:

3 In the day when the keepers of the house shall tremble, and the strong men shall bow themselves, and the grinders cease because they are few, and those that look out of the windows be darkened,

4 And the doors shall be shut in the streets, when the sound of the grinding is low, and he shall rise up at the voice of the bird, and all the daughters of musick shall be brought low;

5 Also when they shall be afraid of that which is high, and fears shall be in the way, and the almond tree shall flourish, and the grasshopper shall be a burden, and desire shall fail: because man goeth to his long home, and the mourners go about the streets:

6 Or ever the silver cord be loosed, or the golden bowl be broken, or the pitcher be broken at the fountain, or the wheel broken at the cistern.

7 Then shall the dust return to the earth as it was: and the spirit shall return unto God who gave it.

8 Vanity of vanities, saith the preacher; all is vanity.

9 And moreover, because the preacher was wise, he still taught the people knowledge; yea, he gave good heed, and sought out, and set in order many proverbs.

10 The preacher sought to find out acceptable words: and that which was written was upright, even words of truth.

11 The words of the wise are as goads, and as nails fastened by the masters of assemblies, which are given from one shepherd.

12 And further, by these, my son, be admonished: of making many books there is no end; and much study is a weariness of the flesh.

13 Let us hear the conclusion of the whole matter: Fear God, and keep his commandments: for this is the whole duty of man.

14 For God shall bring every work into judgment, with every secret thing, whether it be good, or whether it be evil.

Isaiah 53:6 KJV

6 All we like sheep have gone astray; we have turned every one to his own way; and the LORD hath laid on him the iniquity of us all.

A description of the depravity of human nature
Psalm 14 King James Version (KJV)

1 The fool hath said in his heart, There is no God. They are corrupt, they have done abominable works, there is none that doeth good.

2 The LORD looked down from heaven upon the children of men, to see if there were any that did understand, and seek God.

3 They are all gone aside, they are all together become filthy: there is none that doeth good, no, not one.

4 Have all the workers of iniquity no knowledge? who eat upMy people as they eat bread, and call not upon the LORD.

5 There were they in great fear: for God is in the generation of the righteous.

6 Ye have shamed the counsel of the poor, because the LORD is his refuge.

7 Oh that the salvation of Israel were come out of Zion! when the LORD bringeth back the captivity of his people, Jacob shall rejoice, and Israel shall be glad.

Signs of the End of This Age
Mark 13:29-37 King James Version (KJV)

29 So ye in like manner, when ye shall see these things come to pass, know that it is nigh, even at the doors.

30 Verily I say unto you, that this generation shall not pass, till all these things be done.

31 Heaven and earth shall pass away: butMy words shall not pass away.

32 But of that day and that hour knoweth no man, no, not the angels which are in heaven, neither the Son, but the Father.

33 Take ye heed, watch and pray: for ye know not when the time is.

34 For the Son of Man is as a man taking a far journey, who left his house, and gave authority to his servants, and to every man his work, and commanded the porter to watch.

35 Watch ye therefore: for ye know not when the master of the house cometh, at even, or at midnight, or at the cockcrowing, or in the morning:

36 Lest coming suddenly he find you sleeping.

37 And what I say unto you I say unto all, Watch.

Understanding and Wisdom
Proverbs James Version (KJV)

1 Hear, ye children, the instruction of a father, and attend to know understanding.

2 For I give you good doctrine, forsake ye not My law.

3 For I was father's son, tender and only beloved in the sight of My mother.

4 He taught me also, and said unto me, Let thine heart retain My words: keep MY commandments, and live.

5 Get wisdom, get understanding: forget it not; neither decline from the words ofMy mouth.

6 Forsake her not, and she shall preserve thee: love her, and she shall keep thee.

7 Wisdom is the principal thing; therefore get wisdom: and with all thy getting get understanding.

Jesus Spoke to the multitudes in parables, such as the Parable of the Sower and Mustard Seed Matthew 13:1-53 King James Version (KJV)

13 The same day went Jesus out of the house, and sat by the sea side.

2 And great multitudes were gathered together unto him, so that He went into a ship, and sat; and the whole multitude stood on the shore.

*3 And He spake many things unto them in parables, saying, Behold, a **sower went forth to sow;***

4 And when he sowed, some seeds fell by the way side, and the fowls came and devoured them up:

5 Some fell upon stony places, where they had not much earth: and forthwith they sprung up, because they had no deepness of earth:

6 And when the sun was up, they were scorched; and because they had no root, they withered away.

7 And some fell among thorns; and the thorns sprung up, and choked them:

8 But other fell into good ground, and brought forth fruit, some an hundredfold, some sixtyfold, some thirtyfold.

9 Who hath ears to hear, let him hear.

10 And the disciples came, and said unto him, Why speakest thou unto them in parables?

11 He answered and said unto them, Because it is given unto you to know the mysteries of the kingdom of heaven, but to them it is not given.

12 For whosoever hath, to him shall be given, and he shall have more abundance: but whosoever hath not, from him shall be taken away even that he hath.

13 Therefore speak I to them in parables: because they seeing see not; and hearing they hear not, neither do they understand.

14 And in them is fulfilled the prophecy of Esaias, which saith, By hearing ye shall hear, and shall not understand; and seeing ye shall see, and shall not perceive:

15 For this people's heart is waxed gross, and their ears are dull of hearing, and their eyes they have closed; lest at any time they should see with their eyes and hear with their ears, and should understand with their heart, and should be converted, and I should heal them.

16 But blessed are your eyes, for they see: and your ears, for they hear.

17 For verily I say unto you, That many prophets and righteous men have desired to see those things which ye see, and have not seen them; and to hear those things which ye hear, and have not heard them.

18 Hear ye therefore the parable of the sower.

19 When any one heareth the word of the kingdom, and understandeth it not, then cometh the wicked one, and catcheth away that which was sown in his heart. This is he which received seed by the way side.

20 But he that received the seed into stony places, the same is he that heareth the word, and anon with joy receiveth it;

21 Yet hath he not root in himself, but dureth for a while: for when tribulation or persecution ariseth because of the word, by and by he is offended.

22 *He also that received seed among the thorns is he that heareth the word; and the care of this world, and the deceitfulness of riches, choke the word, and he becometh unfruitful.*

23 *But he that received seed into the good ground is he that heareth the word, and understandeth it; which also beareth fruit, and bringeth forth, some an hundredfold, some sixty, some thirty.*

24 *Another parable put he forth unto them, saying, The kingdom of heaven is likened unto a man which sowed good seed in his field:*

25 *But while men slept, his enemy came and sowed tares among the wheat, and went his way.*

26 *But when the blade was sprung up, and brought forth fruit, then appeared the tares also.*

27 *So the servants of the householder came and said unto him, Sir, didst not thou sow good seed in thy field? from whence then hath it tares?*

28 *He said unto them, An enemy hath done this. The servants said unto him, Wilt thou then that we go and gather them up?*

29 *But He said, Nay; lest while ye gather up the tares, ye root up also the wheat with them.*

30 Let both grow together until the harvest: and in the time of harvest I will say to the reapers, Gather ye together first the tares, and bind them in bundles to burn them: but gather the wheat into my barn.

31 Another parable put He forth unto them, saying, The kingdom of heaven is like to a **grain of mustard seed**, which a man took, and sowed in his field:

32 Which indeed is the least of all seeds: but when it is grown, it is the greatest among herbs, and becometh a tree, so that the birds of the air come and lodge in the branches thereof.

33 Another parable spake He unto them; The kingdom of heaven is like unto leaven, which a woman took, and hid in three measures of meal, till the whole was leavened.

34 All these things spake Jesus unto the multitude in parables; and without a parable spake He not unto them:

35 That it might be fulfilled which was spoken by the prophet, saying, I will openMy mouth in parables; I will utter things which have been kept secret from the foundation of the world.

36 Then Jesus sent the multitude away, and went into the house: and his disciples came unto him, saying, Declare unto us the parable of the tares of the field.

37 He answered and said unto them, He that soweth the good seed is the Son of man;

38 The field is the world; the good seed are the children of the kingdom; but the tares are the children of the wicked one;

39 The enemy that sowed them is the devil; the harvest is the end of the world; and the reapers are the angels.

40 As therefore the tares are gathered and burned in the fire; so shall it be in the end of this world.

41 The Son of man shall send forth his angels, and they shall gather out of his kingdom all things that offend, and them which do iniquity;

42 And shall cast them into a furnace of fire: there shall be wailing and gnashing of teeth.

43 Then shall the righteous shine forth as the sun in the kingdom of their Father. Who hath ears to hear, let him hear.

44 Again, the kingdom of heaven is like unto treasure hid in a field; the which when a man hath found, he hideth, and for joy thereof goeth and selleth all that he hath, and buyeth that field.

45 Again, the kingdom of heaven is like unto a merchant man, seeking goodly pearls:

46 Who, when he had found one pearl of great price, went and sold all that he had, and bought it.

47 Again, the kingdom of heaven is like unto a net, that was cast into the sea, and gathered of every kind:

48 Which, when it was full, they drew to shore, and sat down, and gathered the good into vessels, but cast the bad away.

49 So shall it be at the end of the world: the angels shall come forth, and sever the wicked from among the just,

50 And shall cast them into the furnace of fire: there shall be wailing and gnashing of teeth.

51 Jesus saith unto them, Have ye understood all these things? They say unto him, Yea, Lord.

52 Then said He unto them, Therefore every scribe which is instructed unto the kingdom of heaven is like unto a man that is an householder, which bringeth forth out of his treasure things new and old.

53 And it came to pass, that when Jesus had finished these parables, He departed thence.

Why You Should Not Mock An Elderly Person Or A Prophet

2 Kings 2:23 And he went up from thence unto Bethel: and as he was going up by the way, there came forth little children out of the city, and mocked him, and said unto him, Go up, thou bald head; go up, thou bald head.

2 Kings 2:24 And he turned back, and looked on them, and cursed them in the name of the LORD. And there came forth two she bears out of the wood, and tare forty and two children of them.

Luke 6:31 And as ye would that men should do to you, do ye also to them likewise.

Illustrative Artwork by

M.E. Cunningham, Kennedy Jasmine Ringgold
(Henry's Great-Granddaughter and student at the
Maryland Institute College of Art), and Henry
L. & Robert H. Green (Henry's Oldest Son)

Wedding at Cana

Illustrative Artwork by M.E. Cunningham

And there came forth two she bears out of the wood....

1 King 2:23-24

Illustrative Artwork by Kennedy Jasmine Ringgold

The Story of Jonah and the Whale

Jonah 1-2

Illustrative Artwork by Kennedy Jasmine Ringgold

Parable of the Sower and Seeds

Matthew 13:1-53 (KJV)

Illustrative Artwork by Kennedy Jasmine Ringgold

Jesus said, "Follow me, and I will make you fishers of men." Matthew 4:19, KJV\

Illustrative Artwork by Kennedy Jasmine Ringgold

Moses Leading the People out of Egypt, Exodus 14 (KJV)

Illustrative Artwork by Kennedy Jasmine Ringgold

Genesis 9:14-15

14 And it shall come to pass, when I bring a cloud over the earth, that the bow shall be seen in the cloud:

15And I will remember my covenant, which is between me and you and every living creature of all flesh; and the waters shall no more become a flood to destroy all flesh.

Illustrative Artwork by Henry Louis and Robert Henry Green

Chapter IV

"The Lord's Prayer"

King James & Gideon Versions

One of my favorite prayers in the Bible is the Lord's Prayer. It is part of the Sermon on the Mount where Jesus was teaching biblical principles. The disciples Matthew and Luke wrote their versions of the Lord's Prayer. Also, the King James Version (KJV) of the Lord's Prayer is slightly different from the Gideon's bible. Jesus said, in Matthew 6:7, *But when ye pray, use not vain repetitions, as the heathen do: for they think that they shall be heard for their much speaking.* He also said in Matthew 6:8, *Be not ye therefore like unto them: for your Father knoweth what things ye have need of, before ye ask him. 9 After this manner therefore pray ye:*

"THE LORD'S PRAYER"
KJV- Matthew 6:9-13

Our Father which art in heaven,
Hallowed be thy name. Thy kingdom come.

Thy will be done in earth, as it is in heaven.
Give us this day our daily bread.
And forgive us our debts, as we forgive our debtors.
And lead us not into temptation, but deliver us from evil: For
thine is the kingdom, and the power, and the glory, forever.
Amen.

I want to point out that the Gideon's, versions says, "your will be done, <u>on earth</u> as it is in heaven" and the King James Version says, "Thy will be done <u>in earth</u>, as it is in heaven". God called the dry land Earth and on earth were the waters; however, above the earth and waters is the firmament which includes the atmosphere and heaven. I always preferred the KJV of the Bible and often wondered what the difference is, if any, between "on earth" and "in earth." I believe "on earth" is just the surface of the earth and "in earth" refers to and includes the atmosphere and beyond. In Genesis the Bible teaches about the formation of the heaven and the earth as follows:

Genesis 1 King James Version (KJV)

1 In the beginning God created the heaven and the earth.

2 And the earth was without form, and void; and darkness was upon the face of the deep. And the Spirit of God moved upon the face of the waters.

3 And God said, Let there be light: and there was light.

4 And God saw the light, that it was good: and God divided the light from the darkness.

5 And God called the light Day, and the darkness HE called Night. And the evening and the morning were the first day.

6 And God said, Let there be a <u>firmament</u> in the <u>midst of the waters, and let it divide the waters from the waters.</u>

7 And God made the <u>firmament</u>, and divided the waters which were under the <u>firmament</u> from the waters which were above the <u>firmament</u>: and it was so.

8 And God called the <u>firmament</u> Heaven. And the evening and the morning were the second day.

9 And God said, Let the waters under the heaven be gathered together unto one place, and let the dry land appear: and it was so.

10 And God called the dry land Earth; and the gathering together of the waters called the Seas: and God saw that it was good.

11 And God said, Let the earth bring forth grass, the herb yielding seed, and the fruit tree yielding fruit after his kind, whose seed is in itself, upon the earth: and it was so.

12 And the earth brought forth grass, and herb yielding seed after his kind, and the tree yielding fruit, whose seed was in itself, after his kind: and God saw that it was good.

13 And the evening and the morning were the third day.

14 And God said, <u>Let there be lights in the firmament of the heaven to divide the day from the night</u>; and let them be for signs, and for seasons, and for days, and years:

15 And let them be for lights in the <u>firmament</u> of the heaven to give light upon the earth: and it was so.

16 And <u>God made two great lights</u>; the greater light to rule the day, and the lesser light to rule the night: HE made the <u>stars</u> also.

17 And God set them in the <u>firmament</u> of the heaven to give light upon the earth,

18 And to rule over the day and over the night, and to divide the light from the darkness: and God saw that it was good.

In Genesis 1:6-8, God said:

6 And God said, Let there be a <u>firmament in the midst of the waters</u>, and let it <u>divide the waters from the</u>

waters. 7 And God made the firmament, and <u>divided the waters</u> which were <u>under the firmament</u> from the <u>waters which were above the firmament</u>: and it was so. 8 And <u>God called the firmament Heaven</u>. And the evening and the morning were the second day."

In Genesis 1:7, "under the firmament" is the atmosphere; however God is also referring to the waters which are above the firmament, which in my opinion refers to the outer space or the universe.

Then in Genesis 1:14-16 KJV) the Bible teaches,

[14] And God said, <u>Let there be lights in the firmament of the heaven to divide the day from the night</u>; and let them be for signs, and for seasons, and for days, and years:

[15] And let them be for lights in the <u>firmament</u> of the heaven to give light upon the earth: and it was so.

[16] And <u>God made two great lights</u>; the greater light to rule the day, and the lesser light to rule the night: HE made the <u>stars</u> also.

[17] And God set them in the <u>firmament</u> of the heaven to give light upon the earth,

In Genesis 1:16, God set the Sun for lights in the firmament for day which is called "the greater light" and the "lesser lights to rule the night" are the Stars, which confirms that God is speaking of the cosmos and universe. Therefore in Genesis 1:7, when God said, "above the firmament" one must conclude He is speaking of things beyond the Sun and the Stars. In view of the above, I would recommend the King James Version of the Lord's Prayer; because it is more inclusive of the universe or Heaven.

Here is a comparison of two version of the Lord's Prayer:

The King James Version of the Bible and The Gideon Bible Version of the Lord's Prayer:

The King James Version of The Lord's Prayer

The prayer as it occurs in Matthew 6:9–13 (KJV)	The prayer as it occurs in Luke 11:2–4 (KJV)
Matthew 6:9 After this manner therefore pray ye: Our Father which art in heaven, Hallowed be thy name.	"**Luke 11:2** And He said unto them, When ye pray, say, Our Father which art in heaven, Hallowed be thy name. Thy kingdom come. Thy will be done, as <u>in</u> heaven, so <u>in</u> earth.
Matthew 6:10 Thy kingdom come. Thy will be done <u>in</u> earth, as it is <u>in</u> heaven.	
Matthew 6:11 Give us this day our daily bread.	**Luke 11:3** Give us day by day our daily bread.
Matthew 6:12 And forgive us our debts, as we forgive our debtors.	**Luke 11:4** And forgive us our sins; for we also forgive every one that is indebted to us.
Matthew 6:13 And lead us not into temptation, but deliver us from evil: For thine is the kingdom, and the power, and the glory, for ever. Amen.	And lead us not into temptation; but deliver us from evil.

The Gideon Bible Version of the Lord's Prayer

The prayer as it occurs in Matthew 6:9–13 (ESV)	The prayer as it occurs in Luke 11:2–4 (ESV)
"Our Father in heaven,	"Father,
hallowed be your name.	hallowed be your name.
Your kingdom come,	Your kingdom come.
your will be done,	your will be done
<u>on</u> earth as it is in heaven.	<u>on</u> earth as it is in heaven.
Give us this day our daily bread,	Give us each day our daily bread,
and forgive us our debts,	and forgive us our sins,
as we also have forgiven our debtors.	for we ourselves forgive everyone who is indebted to us.
And lead us not into temptation,	And lead us not into temptation."
but deliver us from evil."	

While the Lord's Prayer is one of my favorite prayers, and it has been written in a number of ways or versions, I love it so much because it always reminds me of what the Bible teaches us in 1 Thessalonians 5:16-17"… to rejoice evermore and pray without ceasing." Also, "In everything give thanks: for this is the will of God in Christ Jesus concerning you." 1 Thessalonians 5:18

Chapter V

"The Story of Noah's Ark"

Genesis Chapter 6 Through Chapter 9

The Bible says, in Hebrew 11:7, "By faith Noah, being warned of God of things not seen as yet, moved with fear, prepared an ark to the saving of his house; by the which He condemned the world, and became heir of the righteousness which is by faith."

The story of Noah is important and I will tell you why at the end of Genesis chapter nine.

In Noah's Ark LORD God Destroyed The Earth Because It Was Filled With Violence, Genesis 6-9

Genesis 6:1 And it came to pass, when men began to multiply on the face of the earth, and daughters were born unto them,

Genesis 6:2 That the sons of God saw the daughters of men that they were fair; and they took them wives of all which they chose.

Genesis 6:3 And the LORD said, My spirit shall not always strive with man, for that he also is flesh: yet his days shall be a hundred and twenty years.

Genesis 6:4 There were giants in the earth in those days; and also after that, when the sons of God came in unto the daughters of man and they bare children to them, the same became mighty men which were of old, men of renown.

Genesis 6:5 And GOD saw that the wickedness of man was great in the earth, and that every imagination of the thoughts of his heart was only evil continually.

Genesis 6:6 And it repented the LORD that HE had made man on the earth, and it grieved him at his heart.

Genesis 6:7 And the LORD said, I will destroy man whom I have created from the face of the earth; both man, and beast, and the creeping thing, and the fowls of the air; for it repenteth me that I have made them.

Genesis 6:8 But Noah found grace in the eyes of the LORD.

Genesis 6:9 These are the generations of Noah: Noah was a just man and perfect in his generations, and Noah walked with God.

Genesis 6:10 And Noah begat three sons, Shem, Ham, and Japheth.

Genesis 6:11 The earth also was corrupt before God, and the earth was filled with violence.

Genesis 6:12 And God looked upon the earth, and, behold, it was corrupt; for all flesh had corrupted his way upon the earth.

Genesis 6:13 And God said unto Noah, The end of all flesh is come before me; for the earth is filled with violence through them; and, behold, I will destroy them with the earth.

Genesis 6:14 Make thee an ark of gopher wood; rooms shalt thou make in the ark, and shalt pitch it within and without with pitch.

Genesis 6:15 And this is the fashion which thou shalt make it of: The length of the ark shall be three hundred cubits, the breadth of it fifty cubits, and the height of it thirty cubits.

Genesis 6:16 A window shalt thou make to the ark, and in a cubit shalt thou finish it above; and the door of the ark shalt thou set in the side thereof; with lower, second, and third stories shalt thou make it.

Genesis 6:17 And, behold, I, even I, do bring a flood of waters upon the earth, to destroy all flesh, wherein is the breath of life, from under heaven; and every thing that is in the earth shall die.

Genesis 6:18 But with thee will I establishMy covenant; and thou shalt come into the ark, thou, and thy sons, and thy wife, and thy sons' wives with thee.

Genesis 6:19 And of every living thing of all flesh, two of every sort shalt thou bring into the ark, to keep them alive with thee; they shall be male and female.

Genesis 6:20 Of fowls after their kind, and of cattle after their kind, of every creeping thing of the earth after his kind, two of every sort shall come unto thee, to keep them alive.

Genesis 6:21 And take thou unto thee of all food that is eaten, and thou shalt gather it to thee; and it shall be for food for thee, and for them.

Genesis 6:22 Thus did Noah; according to all that God commanded him, so did he.

Genesis 7:1 And the LORD said unto Noah, Come thou and all thy house into the ark; for thee have I seen righteous before me in this generation.

Genesis 7:2 Of every clean beast thou shalt take to thee by sevens, the male and his female: and of beasts that are not clean by two, the male and his female.

Genesis 7:3 Of fowls also of the air by sevens, the male and the female; to keep seed alive upon the face of all the earth.

Genesis 7:4 For yet seven days, and I will cause it to rain upon the earth forty days and forty nights; and every living substance that I have made will I destroy from off the face of the earth.

Genesis 7:5 And Noah did according unto all that the LORD commanded him.

Genesis 7:6 And Noah was six hundred years old when the flood of waters was upon the earth.

Genesis 7:7 And Noah went in, and his sons, and his wife, and his sons' wives with him, into the ark, because of the waters of the flood.

Genesis 7:8 Of clean beasts, and of beasts that are not clean, and of fowls, and of everything that creepeth upon the earth,

Genesis 7:9 There went in two and two unto Noah into the ark, the male and the female, as God had commanded Noah.

Genesis 7:10 And it came to pass after seven days, that the waters of the flood were upon the earth.

Genesis 7:11 In the six hundredth year of Noah's life, in the second month, the seventeenth day of the month, the same day were all the fountains of the great deep broken up, and the windows of heaven were opened.

Genesis 7:12 And the rain was upon the earth forty days and forty nights.

Genesis 7:13 In the selfsame day entered Noah, and Shem, and Ham, and Japheth, the sons of Noah, and Noah's wife, and the three wives of his sons with them, into the ark;

Genesis 7:14 They, and every beast after his kind, and all the cattle after their kind, and every creeping thing that creepeth upon the earth after his kind, and every fowl after his kind, every bird of every sort.

Genesis 7:15 And they went in unto Noah into the ark, two and two of all flesh, wherein is the breath of life.

Genesis 7:16 And they that went in, went in male and female of all flesh, as God had commanded him: and the LORD shut him in.

Genesis 7:17 And the flood was forty days upon the earth; and the waters increased, and bare up the ark, and it was lift up above the earth.

Genesis 7:18 And the waters prevailed, and were increased greatly upon the earth; and the ark went upon the face of the waters.

Genesis 7:19 And the waters prevailed exceedingly upon the earth; and all the high hills, that were under the whole heaven, were covered.

Genesis 7:20 Fifteen cubits upward did the waters prevail; and the mountains were covered.

Genesis 7:21 And all flesh died that moved upon the earth, both of fowl, and of cattle, and of beast, and of every creeping thing that creepeth upon the earth, and every man:

Genesis 7:22 All in whose nostrils was the breath of life, of all that was in the dry land, died.

Genesis 7:23 And every living substance was destroyed which was upon the face of the ground, both man, and cattle, and the creeping things, and the fowl of the heaven; and they were destroyed from the earth: and Noah only remained alive, and they that were with him in the ark.

Genesis 7:24 And the waters prevailed upon the earth an hundred and fifty days.

Genesis 8:1 And God remembered Noah, and every living thing, and all the cattle that was with him in the ark: and God made a wind to pass over the earth, and the waters asswaged;

Genesis 8:2 The fountains also of the deep and the windows of heaven were stopped, and the rain from heaven was restrained

Genesis 8:3 And the waters returned from off the earth continually: and after the end of the hundred and fifty days the waters were abated.

Genesis 8:4 And the ark rested in the seventh month, on the seventeenth day of the month, upon the mountains of Ararat.

Genesis 8:5 And the waters decreased continually until the tenth month: in the tenth month, on the first day of the month, were the tops of the mountains seen.

Genesis 8:6 And it came to pass at the end of forty days, that Noah opened the window of the ark which he had made:

Genesis 8:7 And he sent forth a raven, which went forth to and fro, until the waters were dried up from off the earth.

Genesis 8:8 Also he sent forth a dove from him, to see if the waters were abated from off the face of the ground;

Genesis 8:9 But the dove found no rest for the sole of her foot, and she returned unto him into the ark, for the waters were on the face of the whole earth: then he put forth his hand, and took her, and pulled her in unto him into the ark.

Genesis 8:10 And he stayed yet other seven days; and again he sent forth the dove out of the ark;

Genesis 8:11 And the dove came in to him in the evening; and, lo, in her mouth was an olive leaf pluckt off: so Noah knew that the waters were abated from off the earth.

Genesis 8:12 And he stayed yet other seven days; and sent forth the dove; which returned not again unto him any more.

Genesis 8:13 And it came to pass in the six hundredth and first year, in the first month, the first day of the month, the waters were dried up from off the earth: and Noah removed the covering of the ark, and looked, and, behold, the face of the ground was dry.

Genesis 8:14 And in the second month, on the seven and twentieth day of the month, was the earth dried.

Genesis 8:15 And God spake unto Noah, saying,

Genesis 8:16 Go forth of the ark, thou, and thy wife, and thy sons, and thy sons' wives with thee.

Genesis 8:17 Bring forth with thee every living thing that is with thee, of all flesh, both of fowl, and of cattle, and of every creeping thing that creepeth upon the earth; that they may breed abundantly in the earth, and be fruitful, and multiply upon the earth.

Genesis 8:18 And Noah went forth, and his sons, and his wife, and his sons' wives with him:

Genesis 8:19 Every beast, every creeping thing, and every fowl, and whatsoever creepeth upon the earth, after their kinds, went forth out of the ark.

Genesis 8:20 And Noah builded an altar unto the LORD; and took of every clean beast, and of every clean fowl, and offered burnt offerings on the altar.

Genesis 8:21 And the LORD smelled a sweet savour; and the LORD said in his heart, I will not again curse the ground any more for man's sake; for the imagination of man's heart is evil from his youth; neither will I again smite any more every thing living, as I have done.

Genesis 8:22 While the earth remaineth, seedtime and harvest, and cold and heat, and summer and winter, and day and night shall not cease.

Genesis 9:1 And God blessed Noah and his sons, and said unto them, Be fruitful, and multiply, and replenish the earth.

Genesis 9:2 And the fear of you and the dread of you shall be upon every beast of the earth, and upon every fowl of the air, upon all that moveth upon the earth, and upon all the fishes of the sea; into your hand are they delivered.

Genesis 9:3 Every moving thing that liveth shall be meat for you; even as the green herb have I given you all things.

Genesis 9:4 But flesh with the life thereof, which is the blood thereof, shall ye not eat.

Genesis 9:5 And surely your blood of your lives will I require; at the hand of every beast will I require it, and at the hand of man; at the hand of every man's brother will I require the life of man.

Genesis 9:6 Whoso sheddeth man's blood, by man shall his blood be shed: for in the image of God made he man.

Genesis 9:7 And you, be ye fruitful, and multiply; bring forth abundantly in the earth, and multiply therein.

Genesis 9:8 And God spake unto Noah, and to his sons with him, saying,

Genesis 9:9 And I, behold, I establish My covenant with you, and with your seed after you;

Genesis 9:10 And with every living creature that is with you, of the fowl, of the cattle, and of every beast of the earth with you; from all that go out of the ark, to every beast of the earth.

Genesis 9:11 And I will establish My covenant with you; neither shall all flesh be cut off any more by the waters of a flood; neither shall there any more be a flood to destroy the earth.

Genesis 9:12 And God said, This is the token of the covenant which I make between me and you and every living creature that is with you, for perpetual generations:

Genesis 9:13 I do set My bow in the cloud, and it shall be for a token of a covenant between me and the earth.

Genesis 9:14 And it shall come to pass, when I bring a cloud over the earth, that the bow shall be seen in the cloud:

Genesis 9:15 And I will remember My covenant, which is between me and you and every living creature of all flesh; and the waters shall no more become a flood to destroy all flesh.

Genesis 9:16 And the bow shall be in the cloud; and I will look upon it, that I may remember the everlasting covenant between God and every living creature of all flesh that is upon the earth.

Genesis 9:17 And God said unto Noah, This is the token of the covenant, which I have established between me and all flesh that is upon the earth.

Genesis 9:18 And the sons of Noah, that went forth of the ark, were Shem, and Ham, and Japheth: and Ham is the father of Canaan.

Genesis 9:19 These are the three sons of Noah: and of them was the whole earth overspread.

Genesis 9:20 And Noah began to be an husbandman, and he planted a vineyard:

Genesis 9:21 And he drank of the wine, and was drunken; and he was uncovered within his tent.

Genesis 9:22 And Ham, the father of Canaan, saw the nakedness of his father, and told his two brethren without.

Genesis 9:23 And Shem and Japheth took a garment, and laid it upon both their shoulders, and went backward, and covered the nakedness of their father; and their faces were backward, and they saw not their father's nakedness.

Genesis 9:24 And Noah awoke from his wine, and knew what his younger son had done unto him.

Genesis 9:25 And he said, Cursed be Canaan; a servant of servants shall he be unto his brethren.

Genesis 9:26 And he said, Blessed be the LORD God of Shem; and Canaan shall be his servant.

Genesis 9:27 God shall enlarge Japheth, and he shall dwell in the tents of Shem; and Canaan shall be his servant.

Genesis 9:28 And Noah lived after the flood three hundred and fifty years.

Genesis 9:29 And all the days of Noah were nine hundred and fifty years: and he died.

While the story of Noah is an allegory and is full of symbols, it is important to remember because if you don't know your past you are doomed to repeat it. In Noah's day and since that time the world has not changed very much. Lack of moral character and degeneration is everywhere. There is still violence including wars and rumors of war. Noah was special and God spared him and his family. As mankind developed from the days of Adam and Eve and their children, the people became more and more depraved and were cruel, evil, and barbaric. Therefore God regretted having created mankind, including the fish of the sea, the animals of the earth and the birds of the sky.

Like I said, Noah and his family were special to Him and found grace before Him and while the earth was filled with violence and corruption, Noah, his wife, and three sons, Shem, Ham and Japheth, the LORD was kind to Noah and his family.

So, God told Noah that HE would destroy the earth, and instructed Noah to build an ark and HE was specific that it would be of gopher wood, fortified with pitch, the length being three hundred cubits, the breadth of it fifty cubits, and the height thirty cubits. God also said the ark would have a window, alongside three levels or stories to house Noah, his family, his son's wives, and a male and female animal of every species from the earth, including cattle, birds and creeping things. Of every clean beast, Noah was instructed to take seven pairs; but of every unclean animal, only two. HE was also told to take seven pairs for the birds of the air.

God told Noah that HE would cause rain to flood the earth for forty days and forty nights, and that all life on the earth would be destroyed. Noah was 600 years old when the rains came, during the seventeenth day of the second month of the year. When the rain came Noah and his family were raised in the ark above the flood which swallowed earth and heaven, the waters having risen 15 cubits up above the earth. The floods prevailed over the earth 150 days.

Afterward, God made the wind to calm the floods, remembering Noah, his family, the ark and the animals therein. The rains slowed down and the floods went away, and the ark was set above the mountains of Ararat on the seventeenth day of the seventh month. The waters continued to subside and on the tenth month until the tops of mountains could be seen.

Noah then sent out a raven and a dove to scout the earth for dry land. The again in seven more days, Noah sent the dove again to scout for dry land, and when the dove returned with an olive leaf in its beak, he knew the floods were receded. Then Noah removed the covering of the ark and saw dry land.

God then spoke to Noah, telling him to be fruitful and multiply on the earth. Noah was so thankful he built an altar and made burnt offerings of every clean animal, which was pleasing to God. Then God said, HE would never again destroy mankind again by flood and made a covenant with Noah, his family, his generations to come and the animals of the earth, that HE would not destroy the earth by flood and as a token of his promise, showed a rainbow representing His covenant with man.

Noah's Faith

Hebrews 11:1-7 King James Version (KJV)

11 Now faith is the substance of things hoped for, the evidence of things not seen.

2 For by it the elders obtained a good report.

3 Through faith we understand that the worlds were framed by the word of God, so that things which are seen were not made of things which do appear.

4 By faith Abel offered unto God a more excellent sacrifice than Cain, by which he obtained witness that he was righteous, God testifying of his gifts: and by it he being dead yet speaketh.

5 By faith Enoch was translated that he should not see death; and was not found, because God had translated him: for before his translation he had this testimony, that he pleased God.

6 But without faith it is impossible to please HIM: for he that cometh to God must believe that HE is, and that HE is a rewarder of them that diligently seek HIM.

7 By faith Noah, being warned of God of things not seen as yet, moved with fear, prepared an ark to the saving of his house; by the which he condemned the world, and became heir of the righteousness which is by faith.

8 By faith Abraham, when he was called to go out into a place which he should after receive for an inheritance, obeyed; and he went out, not knowing whither he went.

9 By faith he sojourned in the land of promise, as in a strange country, dwelling in tabernacles with Isaac and Jacob, the heirs with him of the same promise:

10 For he looked for a city which hath foundations, whose builder and maker is God.

11 Through faith also Sara herself received strength to conceive seed, and was delivered of a child when she was past age, because she judged him faithful who had promised.

Today, mankind has not heeded the warnings of God just like in Noah's day and mankind is destroying the earth and global warming is wrecking havoc on the earth. There is flooding everywhere, extreme drought causing multiple fire in many states, 80% of the sea animals are gone, the honey is almost extinct due to pesticides and without the honey bee to pollinate our vegetables and fruit will be gone and according to Einstein, after the bees are dead, eight years later, so will mankind. Mankind are so greedy, they don't care. Also, more and more children are being born with Autism, due to an unknown cause, (which I believe they know what causes it), mankind is causing its own extinction. The odds of being born with Autism is now 1 in 68.

Chapter VI

"The Sermon On The Mount"

The Beatitudes

Matthew Chapter 5-7

The beatitudes are the teachings of Jesus Christ about spiritual gifts and principles or values that we must reflect on and have the free will to live by. At the time, His audience was His disciples and the multitudes who were their followers who had heard of His preaching and healings. However, His teachings were timeless and were about how we should conduct ourselves in order to live a good Christian life. During this Sermon on the Mount, Jesus Christ gave new meaning or interpretation to the law from the Old Testament as was prophesied by Isaiah Chapter 11, verses 1 through 4.

Isaiah 11:1-4 KJV

1 And there shall come forth a rod out of the stem of Jesse, and a Branch shall grow out of his roots:

2 And the spirit of the LORD shall rest upon Him, the spirit of wisdom and understanding, the spirit of

counsel and might, the spirit of knowledge and of the fear of the LORD;

3 And shall make Him of quick understanding in the fear of the LORD: and He shall not judge after the sight of his eyes, neither reprove after the hearing of his ears:

4 But with righteousness shall He judge the poor, and reprove with equity for the meek of the earth: and shall smite the earth: with the rod of his mouth, and with the breath of his lips shall He slay the wicked.

Isaiah prophesied that the Messiah (Jesus Christ), would be an offspring of Jesse, the father of David and that the spirit of the LORD shall rest upon Him, the spirit of wisdom and understanding, the spirit of counsel and might, the spirit of knowledge and of the fear of the LORD and that with righteousness shall He judge the poor, and reprove with equity for the meek of the earth: and He shall smite the earth: with the rod of his mouth, and with the breath of his lips shall He slay the wicked. (Isaiah 11:2-3 KJV) Jesus used all of these spiritual gifts when He gave his Sermon on the Mount.

Background Before the Sermon on the Mount

After Jesus had spent forty days and nights in the desert being tempted by the devil, the devil left Him and angels came and ministered to Him. (Matthew 4:1-11 KJV) Jesus heard that John the Baptist was put in prison, He left for Galilee. Then after leaving Nazareth He dwelt in Capernaun near the sea coast, in the border of Zabulon and Nephthalim which was prophesied by Esaias who said that in this land of Zabulon, on the land of Nephthalim beyond Jordan, Galilee of the Gentiles, the people sat in darkness saw great light, and to them which sat in darkness saw great light and shadow of death light is sprung up and "From that time, Jesus began to preach, and said, "Repent for the kingdom of heaven is at hand." (Matthew 4:13-17 KJV) Then as Jesus was walking by the sea of Galilee, He saw two brothers, Simon called Peter, and Andrew casting a net into the sea for they were fishers. Jesus said to his first recruit of disciples, "Follow me, and I will make you fishers of men." (Matthew 4:19, KJV) And in Matthew chapter 4 verse 22, it states, "And they immediately left the ship and their father, and followed Him."

Jesus became famous throughout Syria when He went about all of Galilee, teaching in their synagogues, and preaching the gospel of the kingdom and healing all manner of sickness and disease among the people and they brought unto Him all sick people with diseases, torments, possessed with devils, mentally sick, palsy; and He healed them. Then multitudes of people began to follow Him from Galilee, Decapolis, Jerusalem, Judaea and even beyond Jordan. (Matthew 4:23-25 KJV) Jesus felt compelled to teach them the gospel of the kingdom to give them an opportunity to, "Repent for the kingdom of heaven is at hand." (Matthew 4:17 KJV) In John 14:6, He said, "I am the way, the truth, and the life: no man cometh unto the Father, but by me." He also said in John 11:25, "I am the resurrection, and the life: he that believeth in me, though he were dead, yet shall he live:"

The Sermon on the Mount

Matthew 5:1 And seeing the multitudes, He went up into a mountain: and when He was set, his disciples came unto Him:

Matthew 5:2 And He opened His mouth, and taught them, saying,

Matthew 5:3 Blessed are the poor in spirit: for theirs is the kingdom of heaven.

Matthew 5:4 Blessed are they that mourn: for they shall be comforted.

Matthew 5:5 Blessed are the meek: for they shall inherit the earth.

Matthew 5:6 Blessed are they which do hunger and thirst after righteousness: for they shall be filled.

Matthew 5:7 Blessed are the merciful: for they shall obtain mercy.

Matthew 5:8 Blessed are the pure in heart: for they shall see God.

Matthew 5:9 Blessed are the peacemakers: for they shall be called the children of God.

Matthew 5:10 Blessed are they which are persecuted for righteousness' sake: for theirs is the kingdom of heaven.

Matthew 5:11 Blessed are ye, when men shall revile you, and persecute you, and shall say all manner of evil against you falsely, for My sake.

Matthew 5:12 Rejoice, and be exceeding glad: for great is your reward in heaven: for so persecuted they the prophets which were before you.

Matthew 5:13 Ye are the salt of the earth: but if the salt have lost his savour, wherewith shall it be salted? it is thenceforth good for nothing, but to be cast out, and to be trodden under foot of men.

Matthew 5:14 Ye are the light of the world. A city that is set on a hill cannot be hid.

Matthew 5:15 Neither do men light a candle, and put it under a bushel, but on a candlestick; and it giveth light unto all that are in the house.

Matthew 5:16 Let your light so shine before men, that they may see your good works, and glorify your Father which is in heaven.

Matthew 5:17 Think not that I am come to destroy the law, or the prophets: I am not come to destroy, but to fulfill.

Matthew 5:18 For verily I say unto you, Till heaven and earth pass, one jot or one tittle shall in no wise pass from the law, till all be fulfilled.

Matthew 5:19 Whosoever therefore shall break one of these least commandments, and shall teach men so, he shall be called the least in the kingdom of heaven: but whosoever shall do and teach them, the same shall be called great in the kingdom of heaven.

Matthew 5:20 For I say unto you, That except your righteousness shall exceed the righteousness of the scribes and Pharisees, ye shall in no case enter into the kingdom of heaven.

Matthew 5:21 Ye have heard that it was said of them of old time, Thou shalt not kill; and whosoever shall kill shall be in danger of the judgment:

Matthew 5:22 But I say unto you, That whosoever is angry with his brother without a cause shall be in danger of the judgment: and whosoever shall say to his brother, Raca, shall be in danger of the council: but whosoever shall say, Thou fool, shall be in danger of hell fire.

Matthew 5:23 Therefore if thou bring thy gift to the altar, and there rememberest that thy brother hath ought against thee;

Matthew 5:24 Leave there thy gift before the altar, and go thy way; first be reconciled to thy brother, and then come and offer thy gift.

Matthew 5:25 Agree with thine adversary quickly, whiles thou art in the way with him; lest at any time the adversary deliver thee to the judge, and the judge deliver thee to the officer, and thou be cast into prison.

Matthew 5:26 Verily I say unto thee, Thou shalt by no means come out thence, till thou hast paid the uttermost farthing.

Matthew 5:27 Ye have heard that it was said by them of old time, Thou shalt not commit adultery:

Matthew 5:28 But I say unto you, That whosoever looketh on a woman to lust after her hath committed adultery with her already in his heart.

Matthew 5:29 And if thy right eye offend thee, pluck it out, and cast it from thee: for it is profitable for thee that one of thy members should perish, and not that thy whole body should be cast into hell.

Matthew 5:30 And if thy right hand offend thee, cut it off, and cast it from thee: for it is profitable for thee that one of thy members should perish, and not that thy whole body should be cast into hell.

Matthew 5:31 It hath been said, Whosoever shall put away his wife, let him give her a writing of divorcement:

Matthew 5:32 But I say unto you, That whosoever shall put away his wife, saving for the cause of fornication, causeth her to commit adultery: and whosoever shall marry her that is divorced committeth adultery.

Matthew 5:33 Again, ye have heard that it hath been said by them of old time, Thou shalt not forswear thyself, but shalt perform.

Matthew 5:34 But I say unto you, Swear not at all; neither by heaven; for it is God's throne:

Matthew 5:35 Nor by the earth; for it is his footstool: neither by Jerusalem; for it is the city of the great King.

Matthew 5:36 Neither shalt thou swear by thy head, because thou canst not make one hair white or black.

Matthew 5:37 But let your communication be, Yea, yea; Nay, nay: for whatsoever is more than these cometh of evil.

Matthew 5:38 Ye have heard that it hath been said, An eye for an eye, and a tooth for a tooth:

Matthew 5:39 But I say unto you, That ye resist not evil: but whosoever shall smite thee on thy right cheek, turn to him the other also.

Matthew 5:40 And if any man will sue thee at the law, and take away thy coat, let him have thy cloak also.

Matthew 5:41 And whosoever shall compel thee to go a mile, go with him twain.

Matthew 5:42 Give to him that asketh thee, and from him that would borrow of thee turn not thou away.

Matthew 5:43 Ye have heard that it hath been said, Thou shalt love thy neighbour, and hate thine enemy.

Matthew 5:44 But I say unto you, Love your enemies, bless them that curse you, do good to them that hate you, and pray for them which despitefully use you, and persecute you;

Matthew 5:45 That ye may be the children of your Father which is in heaven: for HE maketh HIS sun to rise on the evil and on the good, and sendeth rain on the just and on the unjust.

Matthew 5:46 For if ye love them which love you, what reward have ye? do not even the publicans the same?

Matthew 5:47 And if ye salute your brethren only, what do ye more than others? do not even the publicans so?

Matthew 5:48 Be ye therefore perfect, even as your Father which is in heaven is perfect.

Matthew 6:1 Take heed that ye do not your alms before men, to be seen of them: otherwise ye have no reward of your Father which is in heaven.

Matthew 6:2 Therefore when thou doest thine alms, do not sound a trumpet before thee, as the hypocrites do in the synagogues and in the streets, that they may have glory of men. Verily I say unto you, They have their reward.

Matthew 6:3 But when thou doest alms, let not thy left hand know what thy right hand doeth:

Matthew 6:4 That thine alms may be in secret: and thy Father which seeth in secret himself shall reward thee openly.

Matthew 6:5 And when thou prayest, thou shalt not be as the hypocrites are: for they love to pray standing in the synagogues and in the corners of the streets, that they may be seen of men. Verily I say unto you, They have their reward.

Matthew 6:6 But thou, when thou prayest, enter into thy closet, and when thou hast shut thy door, pray to thy Father which is in secret; and thy Father which seeth in secret shall reward thee openly.

Matthew 6:7 But when ye pray, use not vain repetitions, as the heathen do: for they think that they shall be heard for their much speaking.

Matthew 6:8 Be not ye therefore like unto them: for your Father knoweth what things ye have need of, before ye ask him.

Matthew 6:9 After this manner therefore pray ye: **Our Father which art in heaven, Hallowed be thy name.**

Matthew 6:10 **Thy kingdom come, Thy will be done in earth, as it is in heaven.**

Matthew 6:11 **Give us this day our daily bread.**

Matthew 6:12 **And forgive us our debts, as we forgive our debtors.**

Matthew 6:13 **And lead us not into temptation, but deliver us from evil: For thine is the kingdom, and the power, and the glory, for ever. Amen.**

Matthew 6:14 For if ye forgive men their trespasses, your heavenly Father will also forgive you:

Matthew 6:15 But if ye forgive not men their trespasses, neither will your Father forgive your trespasses.

Matthew 6:16 Moreover when ye fast, be not, as the hypocrites, of a sad countenance: for they disfigure their faces, that they may appear unto men to fast. Verily I say unto you, They have their reward.

Matthew 6:17 But thou, when thou fastest, anoint thine head, and wash thy face;

Matthew 6:18 That thou appear not unto men to fast, but unto thy Father which is in secret: and thy Father, which seeth in secret, shall reward thee openly.

Matthew 6:19 Lay not up for yourselves treasures upon earth, where moth and rust doth corrupt, and where thieves break through and steal:

Matthew 6:20 But lay up for yourselves treasures in heaven, where neither moth nor rust doth corrupt, and where thieves do not break through nor steal:

Matthew 6:21 For where your treasure is, there will your heart be also.

Matthew 6:22 The light of the body is the eye: if therefore thine eye be single, thy whole body shall be full of light.

Matthew 6:23 But if thine eye be evil, thy whole body shall be full of darkness. If therefore the light that is in thee be darkness, how great is that darkness!

Matthew 6:24 No man can serve two masters: for either he will hate the one, and love the other; or else he will hold to the one, and despise the other. Ye cannot serve God and mammon.

Matthew 6:25 Therefore I say unto you, Take no thought for your life, what ye shall eat, or what ye shall drink; nor yet for your body, what ye shall put on. Is not the life more than meat, and the body than raiment?

Matthew 6:26 Behold the fowls of the air: for they sow not, neither do they reap, nor gather into barns; yet your heavenly Father feedeth them. Are ye not much better than they?

Matthew 6:27 Which of you by taking thought can add one cubit unto his stature?

Matthew 6:28 And why take ye thought for raiment? Consider the lilies of the field, how they grow; they toil not, neither do they spin:

Matthew 6:29 And yet I say unto you, That even Solomon in all his glory was not arrayed like one of these.

Matthew 6:30 Wherefore, if God so clothe the grass of the field, which to day is, and to morrow is cast into the oven, shall he not much more clothe you, O ye of little faith?

Matthew 6:31 Therefore take no thought, saying, What shall we eat? or, What shall we drink? or, Wherewithal shall we be clothed?

Matthew 6:32 (For after all these things do the Gentiles seek:) for your heavenly Father knoweth that ye have need of all these things.

Matthew 6:33 But seek ye first the kingdom of God, and his righteousness; and all these things shall be added unto you.

Matthew 6:34 Take therefore no thought for the morrow: for the morrow shall take thought for the things of itself. Sufficient unto the day is the evil thereof.

Matthew 7:1 Judge not, that ye be not judged.

Matthew 7:2 For with what judgment ye judge, ye shall be judged: and with what measure ye mete, it shall be measured to you again.

Matthew 7:3 And why beholdest thou the mote that is in thy brother's eye, but considerest not the beam that is in thine own eye?

Matthew 7:4 Or how wilt thou say to thy brother, Let me pull out the mote out of thine eye; and, behold, a beam is in thine own eye?

Matthew 7:5 Thou hypocrite, first cast out the beam out of thine own eye; and then shalt thou see clearly to cast out the mote out of thy brother's eye.

Matthew 7:6 Give not that which is holy unto the dogs, neither cast ye your pearls before swine, lest they trample them under their feet, and turn again and rend you.

Matthew 7:7 Ask, and it shall be given you; seek, and ye shall find; knock, and it shall be opened unto you:

Matthew 7:8 For every one that asketh receiveth; and he that seeketh findeth; and to him that knocketh it shall be opened.

Matthew 7:9 Or what man is there of you, whom if his son ask *bread*, will he give him a stone?

Matthew 7:10 Or if he ask a fish, will he give him a serpent?

Matthew 7:11 If ye then, being evil, know how to give good gifts unto your children, how much more shall your Father which is in heaven give good things to them that ask him?

Matthew 7:12 Therefore all things whatsoever ye would that men should do to you, do ye even so to them: for this is the law and the prophets.

Matthew 7:13 Enter ye in at the strait gate: for wide is the gate, and broad is the way, that leadeth to destruction, and many there be which go in thereat:

Matthew 7:14 Because strait is the gate, and narrow is the way, which leadeth unto life, and few there be that find it.

Matthew 7:15 Beware of false prophets, which come to you in sheep's clothing, but inwardly they are ravening wolves.

Matthew 7:16 Ye shall know them by their fruits. Do men gather grapes of thorns, or figs of thistles?

Matthew 7:17 Even so every good tree bringeth forth good fruit; but a corrupt tree bringeth forth evil fruit.

Matthew 7:18 A good tree cannot bring forth evil fruit, neither can a corrupt tree bring forth good fruit.

Matthew 7:19 Every tree that bringeth not forth good fruit is hewn down, and cast into the fire.

Matthew 7:20 Wherefore by their fruits ye shall know them.

Matthew 7:21 Not every one that saith unto me, Lord, Lord, shall enter into the kingdom of heaven; but he that doeth the will of My Father which is in heaven.

Matthew 7:22 Many will say to me in that day, Lord, Lord, have we not prophesied in thy name? and in thy name have cast out devils? and in thy name done many wonderful works?

Matthew 7:23 And then will I profess unto them, I never knew you: depart from me, ye that work iniquity.

Matthew 7:24 Therefore whosoever heareth these sayings of mine, and doeth them, I will liken him unto a wise man, which built his house upon a rock:

Matthew 7:25 And the rain descended, and the floods came, and the winds blew, and beat upon that house; and it fell not: for it was founded upon a rock.

Matthew 7:26 And every one that heareth these sayings of mine, and doeth them not, shall be likened unto a foolish man, which built his house upon the sand:

Matthew 7:27 And the rain descended, and the floods came, and the winds blew, and beat upon that house; and it fell: and great was the fall of it.

Matthew 7:28 And it came to pass, when Jesus had ended these sayings, the people were astonished at his doctrine:

Matthew 7:29 For He taught them as one having authority, and not as the scribes.

Saint Augustine, was a brilliant scholar of the Bible whose commentaries gave clarity and depth to the Beatitudes of the Sermon on the Mount which transcends the ages. Saint Augustine expressed in one of his commentaries that the "The New Testament is hidden in the Old and the Old is manifest in the New." (Saint Augustine of Hippo, *Quaestiones in Heptateuchum, 2, 73: PL 34, 623*). According to Steven Jonathan Rummelsburg, a renowned commentator, Saint Augustine believed that the first seven Beatitudes are the principle rules of the conduct upon which Jesus based this entire Sermon. Saint Augustine also believed that in the first seven Beatitudes we have a free will choice to follow, however the eight Beatitude is done to us as a consequence of choosing the first seven Beatitudes.

The Beatitudes

1. Matthew 5:3 Blessed are the poor in spirit: for theirs is the kingdom of heaven.

2. Matthew 5:4 Blessed are they that mourn: for they shall be comforted.

3. Matthew 5:5 Blessed are the meek: for they shall inherit the earth.

4. Matthew 5:6 Blessed are they which do hunger and thirst after righteousness: for they shall be filled.

5. Matthew 5:7 Blessed are the merciful: for they shall obtain mercy.

6. Matthew 5:8 Blessed are the pure in heart: for they shall see God.

7. Matthew 5:9 Blessed are the peacemakers: for they shall be called the children of God.

8. Matthew 5:10 Blessed are they which are persecuted for righteousness' sake: for theirs is the kingdom of heaven.

According to Rummelsburg, Saint Augustine clearly demonstrated that Christ "unveiled the law hidden in the Old Testament" when He identified the relationship between the Beatitudes, virtues and the gifts of the Holy Spirit that had been previously identified by the prophet Isaiah. At Isaiah 11:2-3, the prophet reveals the coming of the Christ when he says, "the spirit of the LORD shall rest upon Him." In this regard, Isaiah tells us of the spirit of wisdom, understanding, the spirit of counsel, might, the spirit of knowledge, and the fear of the LORD. Rummelsburg demonstrates that "Christ came to fulfill the law and the prophets." Likewise, Rummelsburg shows that in the Beatitudes, Christ revealed the law hidden in the Isaiah's account of those seven operative principles of the Holy Spirit.

Chapter VII

"Water & Blood & Bread in the Bible"

The Bible speaks on the subject of water, blood and bread on many occasions. Water is essential for life. The blood that runs through our veins is essential for life and bread which represent food or sustenance is needed for life. While these things are essential for life, Jesus came so that we may have everlasting life. In John 6:35, Jesus said, "I am the bread of life: he that cometh to me shall never hunger; and he that believeth on Me shall never thirst."

Even before there was anything; light, sun or moon, earth, plants, living creatures or anything else, there was water. In this chapter, includes some of the instances that I believe are important to remember regarding water, blood and bread:

Genesis, Chapter 1, The Creation

1 In the beginning God created the heaven and the earth.

2 And the earth was without form, and void; and darkness was upon the face of the deep. And the Spirit of God moved upon the face of the waters.

3 And God said, Let there be light: and there was light.

4 And God saw the light, that it was good: and God divided the light from the darkness.

5 And God called the light Day, and the darkness HE called Night. And the evening and the morning were the first day.

6 And God said, Let there be a firmament in the midst of the waters, and let it divide the waters from the waters.

7 And God made the firmament, and divided the waters which were under the firmament from the waters which were above the firmament: and it was so.

8 And God called the firmament Heaven. And the evening and the morning were the second day.

9 And God said, Let the waters under the heaven be gathered together unto one place, and let the dry land appear: and it was so.

10 And God called the dry land Earth; and the gathering together of the waters called HE Seas: and God saw that it was good.

11 And God said, Let the earth bring forth grass, the herb yielding seed, and the fruit tree yielding fruit after his kind, whose seed is in itself, upon the earth: and it was so.

12 And the earth brought forth grass, and herb yielding seed after his kind, and the tree yielding fruit, whose seed was in itself, after his kind: and God saw that it was good.

13 And the evening and the morning were the third day.

14 And God said, Let there be lights in the firmament of the heaven to divide the day from the night; and let them be for signs, and for seasons, and for days, and years:

15 And let them be for lights in the firmament of the heaven to give light upon the earth: and it was so.

16 And God made two great lights; the greater light to rule the day, and the lesser light to rule the night: HE made the stars also.

17 And God set them in the firmament of the heaven to give light upon the earth,

18 And to rule over the day and over the night, and to divide the light from the darkness: and God saw that it was good.

19 And the evening and the morning were the fourth day.

20 And God said, Let the waters bring forth abundantly the moving creature that hath life, and fowl that may fly above the earth in the open firmament of heaven.

21 And God created great whales, and every living creature that moveth, which the waters brought forth abundantly, after their kind, and every winged fowl after his kind: and God saw that it was good.

22 And God blessed them, saying, Be fruitful, and multiply, and fill the waters in the seas, and let fowl multiply in the earth.

God also used that same water which HE created and His spirit moved upon the face of the waters, to destroy the earth in the story of Noah.

Genesis 6 – The Story of Noah

1 And it came to pass, when men began to multiply on the face of the earth, and daughters were born unto them,

2 That the sons of God saw the daughters of men that they were fair; and they took them wives of all which they chose.

3 And the LORD said, My spirit shall not always strive with man, for that he also is flesh: yet his days shall be an hundred and twenty years.

4 There were giants in the earth in those days; and also after that, when the sons of God came in unto the daughters of men, and they bare children to them, the same became mighty men which were of old, men of renown.

5 And God saw that the wickedness of man was great in the earth, and that every imagination of the thoughts of his heart was only evil continually.

6 And it repented the LORD that HE had made man on the earth, and it grieved him at his heart.

7 And the LORD said, I will destroy man whom I have created from the face of the earth; both man, and beast, and the creeping thing, and the fowls of the air; for it repenteth me that I have made them.

8 But Noah found grace in the eyes of the LORD.

9 These are the generations of Noah: Noah was a just man and perfect in his generations, and Noah walked with God.

10 And Noah begat three sons, Shem, Ham, and Japheth.

11 The earth also was corrupt before God, and the earth was filled with violence.

12 And God looked upon the earth, and, behold, it was corrupt; for all flesh had corrupted his way upon the earth.

13 And God said unto Noah, The end of all flesh is come before me; for the earth is filled with violence through them; and, behold, I will destroy them with the earth.

14 Make thee an ark of gopher wood; rooms shalt thou make in the ark, and shalt pitch it within and without with pitch.

15 And this is the fashion which thou shalt make it of: The length of the ark shall be three hundred cubits, the breadth of it fifty cubits, and the height of it thirty cubits.

16 A window shalt thou make to the ark, and in a cubit shalt thou finish it above; and the door of the ark shalt thou set in the side thereof; with lower, second, and third stories shalt thou make it.

17 And, behold, I, even I, do bring a flood of waters upon the earth, to destroy all flesh, wherein is the breath of life, from under heaven; and every thing that is in the earth shall die.

18 But with thee will I establish My covenant; and thou shalt come into the ark, thou, and thy sons, and thy wife, and thy sons' wives with thee.

19 And of every living thing of all flesh, two of every sort shalt thou bring into the ark, to keep them alive with thee; they shall be male and female.

20 Of fowls after their kind, and of cattle after their kind, of every creeping thing of the earth after his kind, two of every sort shall come unto thee, to keep them alive.

21 And take thou unto thee of all food that is eaten, and thou shalt gather it to thee; and it shall be for food for thee, and for them.

22 Thus did Noah; according to all that God commanded him, so did he.

Isaiah 55:1 King James Version (KJV)

55 Ho, every one that thirsteth, come ye to the waters,....

Jeremiah 2:13 King James Version (KJV)

13 For my people have committed two evils; they have forsaken Me the fountain of living waters, and hewed them out cisterns, broken cisterns, that can hold no water.

Matthew 10:42 King James Version (KJV)

42 And whosoever shall give to drink unto one of these little ones a cup of cold water only in the name of a disciple, verily I say unto you, he shall in no wise lose his reward.

John 1:26-28 King James Version (KJV)

26 John answered them, saying, I baptize with water: but there standeth one among you, whom ye know not;

John 7:38King James Version (KJV)

38 He that believeth on me, as the scripture hath said, out of his belly shall flow rivers of living water.

Revelation 22:17 King James Version (KJV)

17 And the Spirit and the bride say, Come. And let him that heareth say, Come. And let him that is athirst come. And whosoever will, let him take the water of life freely.

The Good Samaritan Woman at the Well
John 4:7-14 King James Version (KJV)

7 There cometh a woman of Samaria to draw water: Jesus saith unto her, Give me to drink.

8 (For his disciples were gone away unto the city to buy meat.)

9 Then saith the woman of Samaria unto him, How is it that thou, being a Jew, askest drink of me, which am a woman of Samaria? for the Jews have no dealings with the Samaritans.

10 Jesus answered and said unto her, If thou knewest the gift of God, and who it is that saith to thee, Give me to drink; thou wouldest have asked of him, and He would have given thee living water.

11 The woman saith unto him, Sir, thou hast nothing to draw with, and the well is deep: from whence then hast thou that living water?

12 Art thou greater than our father Jacob, which gave us the well, and drank thereof himself, and his children, and his cattle?

13 Jesus answered and said unto her, Whosoever drinketh of this water shall thirst again:

14 But whosoever drinketh of the water that I shall give him shall never thirst; but the water that I shall give him shall be in him a well of water springing up into everlasting life.

Jesus Walked on the Water
Matthew 14:26-32King James Version (KJV)

26 And when the disciples saw him walking on the sea, they were troubled, saying, It is a spirit; and they cried out for fear.

27 But straightway Jesus spake unto them, saying, Be of good cheer; it is I; be not afraid.

28 And Peter answered him and said, Lord, if it be thou, bid me come unto thee on the water.

29 And He said, Come. And when Peter was come down out of the ship, He walked on the water, to go to Jesus.

30 But when he saw the wind boisterous, he was afraid; and beginning to sink, he cried, saying, Lord, save me.

31 And immediately Jesus stretched forth his hand, and caught him, and said unto him, O thou of little faith, wherefore didst thou doubt?

32 And when they were come into the ship, the wind ceased.

Water and Physical and Spiritual Birth, John 3:1-5

From conception a baby develops and grow in what is essentially a sack of water inside the womb of the mother. Then nine months later when the woman goes into labor, the water break so the baby can be born and breathe the breath of life.

A child must be born physically before a spiritual birth comes. In John 3, Nicodemus, a ruler of the Jews questioned Jesus about this process.

John 3:1-5

1 There was a man of the Pharisees, named Nicodemus, a ruler of the Jews:

2 The same came to Jesus by night, and said unto him, Rabbi, we know that thou art a teacher come from God: for no man can do these miracles that thou doest, except God be with him.

3 Jesus answered and said unto him, Verily, verily, I say unto thee, Except a man be born again, he cannot see the kingdom of God.

4 Nicodemus saith unto him, How can a man be born when he is old? can he enter the second time into his mother's womb, and be born?

5 Jesus answered, Verily, verily, I say unto thee, Except a man be born of water and of the Spirit, he cannot enter into the kingdom of God.

Jesus Walks on the Sea, Matthew 14:22-33

22 And straightway Jesus constrained His disciples to get into a ship, and to go before Him unto the other side, while He sent the multitudes away.

23 And when He had sent the multitudes away, He went up into a mountain apart to pray: and when the evening was come, He was there alone.

24 But the ship was now in the midst of the sea, tossed with waves: for the wind was contrary.

25 And in the fourth watch of the night Jesus went unto them, walking on the sea.

26 And when the disciples saw him walking on the sea, they were troubled, saying, It is a spirit; and they cried out for fear.

27 But straightway Jesus spake unto them, saying, Be of good cheer; it is I; be not afraid.

28 And Peter answered him and said, Lord, if it be thou, bid me come unto thee on the water.

29 And He said, Come. And when Peter was come down out of the ship, he walked on the water, to go to Jesus.

30 But when he saw the wind boisterous, he was afraid; and beginning to sink, he cried, saying, Lord, save me.

31 And immediately Jesus stretched forth his hand, and caught him, and said unto him, O thou of little faith, wherefore didst thou doubt?

32 And when they were come into the ship, the wind ceased.

33 Then they that were in the ship came and worshipped him, saying, Of a truth thou art the Son of God.

Jonah 1-2 - The Story of Jonah and the Whale
Chapter 1

Jonah rebels from God's mission

1 Now the word of the LORD came unto Jonah the son of Amittai, saying,

2 Arise, go to Nineveh, that great city, and cry against it; for their wickedness is come up before me.

3 But Jonah rose up to flee unto Tarshish from the presence of the LORD, and went down to Joppa; and he found a ship going to Tarshish: so he paid the fare thereof, and went down into it, to go with them unto Tarshish from the presence of the LORD.

4 But the LORD sent out a great wind into the sea, and there was a mighty tempest in the sea, so that the ship was like to be broken.

5 Then the mariners were afraid, and cried every man unto his god, and cast forth the wares that were in the ship into the sea, to lighten it of them. But Jonah was gone down into the sides of the ship; and He lay, and was fast asleep.

6 So the shipmaster came to him, and said unto him, What meanest thou, O sleeper? arise, call upon thy God, if so be that God will think upon us, that we perish not.

7 And they said every one to his fellow, Come, and let us cast lots, that we may know for whose cause this evil is upon us. So they cast lots, and the lot fell upon Jonah.

8 Then said they unto him, Tell us, we pray thee, for whose cause this evil is upon us; What is thine occupation? and whence comest thou? what is thy country? and of what people art thou?

9 And He said unto them, I am an Hebrew; and I fear the LORD, the God of heaven, which hath made the sea and the dry land.

10 Then were the men exceedingly afraid, and said unto him, Why hast thou done this? For the men knew that he fled from the presence of the LORD, because he had told them. 11 Then said they unto Him, What shall we do unto thee, that the sea may be calm unto us? for the sea wrought, and was tempestuous.

12 And He said unto them, Take me up, and cast me forth into the sea; so shall the sea be calm unto you: for I know that for My sake this great tempest is upon you.

13 Nevertheless the men rowed hard to bring it to the land; but they could not: for the sea wrought, and was tempestuous against them.

14 Wherefore they cried unto the LORD, and said, We beseech thee, O LORD, we beseech thee, let us not perish for this man's life, and lay not upon us innocent blood: for thou, O LORD, hast done as it pleased thee.

15 So they took up Jonah, and cast him forth into the sea: and the sea ceased from her raging. 16 Then the men feared the LORD exceedingly, and offered a sacrifice unto the LORD, and made vows.

17 Now the LORD had prepared a great fish to swallow up Jonah. And Jonah was in the belly of the fish three days and three nights.

Jonah and the Whale
Chapter 2

1 Then Jonah prayed unto the LORD his God out of the fish's belly,

2 And said, I cried by reason of mine affliction unto the LORD, and he heard me; out of the belly of hell cried I, and thou heardest my voice.

3 For thou hadst cast me into the deep, in the midst of the seas; and the floods compassed me about: all thy billows and thy waves passed over me.

4 Then I said, I am cast out of thy sight; yet I will look again toward thy holy temple.

5 The waters compassed me about, even to the soul: the depth closed me round about, the weeds were wrapped about my head.

6 I went down to the bottoms of the mountains; the earth with her bars was about me for ever: yet hast thou brought up my life from corruption, O LORD my God.

7 When my soul fainted within me I remembered the LORD: and my prayer came in unto thee, into thine holy temple.

8 They that observe lying vanities forsake their own mercy.

9 But I will sacrifice unto thee with the voice of thanksgiving; I will pay that that I have vowed. Salvation is of the LORD.

10 And the LORD spake unto the fish, and it vomited out Jonah upon the dry land.

Exodus

You should definitely read the entire Book of Exodus (Exodus 1-40, KJV). It is the next book after Genesis or the second book in the Old Testament. Exodus tells the story of the migration of the children of Israel out of Egypt away from slavery and oppression by the King of Egypt or Pharaoh. Moses is the pivotal character who is chosen by God to free God's chosen people of Israel and lead them through the wilderness to Mount Sinai. There are trials and tribulations for the people of Israel as they journey across the desert for 40 years, however God provides for them.

In Exodus, Chapter 2, God uses water as a means of deliverance for Moses when he was just an infant. When the Pharaoh's daughter, found the baby in the reeds of the Nile river, she took him home to raise him and called him Moses.

Exodus 2:1-10King James Version (KJV)

1 And there went a man of the house of Levi, and took to wife a daughter of Levi.

2 And the woman conceived, and bare a son: and when she saw him that he was a goodly child, she hid him three months.

3 And when she could not longer hide him, she took for him an ark of bulrushes, and daubed it with slime and with pitch, and put the child therein; and she laid it in the flags by the river's brink.

4 And his sister stood afar off, to wit what would be done to him.

5 And the daughter of Pharaoh came down to wash herself at the river; and her maidens walked along by the river's side; and when she saw the ark among the flags, she sent her maid to fetch it.

6 And when she had opened it, she saw the child: and, behold, the babe wept. And she had compassion on him, and said, This is one of the Hebrews' children.

7 Then said his sister to Pharaoh's daughter, Shall I go and call to thee a nurse of the Hebrew women, that she may nurse the child for thee?

8 And Pharaoh's daughter said to her, Go. And the maid went and called the child's mother.

9 And Pharaoh's daughter said unto her, Take this child away, and nurse it for me, and I will give thee thy wages. And the women took the child, and nursed it.

10 And the child grew, and she brought him unto Pharaoh's daughter, and he became her son. And she called his name Moses: and she said, Because I drew him out of the water.

In Exodus 14, Moses in the Exodus of the Israelites out of Egypy, Crossing the Red Sea. God uses water again when He parts the Red Sea to rescue the Israelites from the army of Pharaoh. Then God used the same sea for both the deliverance of His people and judgment on the Egyptian army.

Exodus, Chapter 14

1 And the LORD spake unto Moses, saying,

2 Speak unto the children of Israel, that they turn and encamp before Pi–hahi'roth, between Migdol and the sea, over against Ba'al–ze'phon: before it shall ye encamp by the sea.

3 For Pharaoh will say of the children of Israel, They are entangled in the land, the wilderness hath shut them in.

4 And I will harden Pharaoh's heart, that he shall follow after them; and I will be honored upon Pharaoh, and upon all his host; that the Egyptians may know that I am the LORD. And they did so.

5 And it was told the king of Egypt that the people fled: and the heart of Pharaoh and of his servants

was turned against the people, and they said, Why have we done this, that we have let Israel go from serving us?

6 And he made ready his chariot, and took his people with him:

7 and he took six hundred chosen chariots, and all the chariots of Egypt, and captains over every one of them.

8 And the LORD hardened the heart of Pharaoh king of Egypt, and he pursued after the children of Israel: and the children of Israel went out with a high hand.

9 But the Egyptians pursued after them, all the horses and chariots of Pharaoh, and his horsemen, and his army, and overtook them encamping by the sea, beside Pi–hahi'roth, before Ba'al–ze'phon.

10 And when Pharaoh drew nigh, the children of Israel lifted up their eyes, and, behold, the Egyptians marched after them; and they were sore afraid: and the children of Israel cried out unto the LORD.

11 And they said unto Moses, Because there were no graves in Egypt, hast thou taken us away to die in the wilderness? wherefore hast thou dealt thus with us, to carry us forth out of Egypt?

12 Is not this the word that we did tell thee in Egypt, saying, Let us alone, that we may serve the Egyptians? For it had been better for us to serve the Egyptians, than that we should die in the wilderness.

13 And Moses said unto the people, Fear ye not, stand still, and see the salvation of the LORD, which he will show to you today: for the Egyptians whom ye have seen today, ye shall see them again no more for ever.

14 The LORD shall fight for you, and ye shall hold your peace.

15 And the LORD said unto Moses, Wherefore criest thou unto me? speak unto the children of Israel, that they go forward:

16 but lift thou up thy rod, and stretch out thine hand over the sea, and divide it: and the children of Israel shall go on dry ground through the midst of the sea.

17 And I, behold, I will harden the hearts of the Egyptians, and they shall follow them: and I will get me honor upon Pharaoh, and upon all his host, upon his chariots, and upon his horsemen.

18 And the Egyptians shall know that I am the LORD, when I have gotten me honor upon Pharaoh, upon his chariots, and upon his horsemen.

19 And the angel of God, which went before the camp of Israel, removed and went behind them; and the pillar of the cloud went from before their face, and stood behind them:

20 and it came between the camp of the Egyptians and the camp of Israel; and it was a cloud and darkness to them, but it gave light by night to these: so that the one came not near the other all the night.

21 And Moses stretched out his hand over the sea; and the LORD caused the sea to go back by a strong east wind all that night, and made the sea dry land, and the waters were divided.

22 And the children of Israel went into the midst of the sea upon the dry ground: Heb. 11.29 and the waters were a wall unto them on their right hand, and on their left.

23 And the Egyptians pursued, and went in after them to the midst of the sea, even all Pharaoh's horses, his chariots, and his horsemen.

24 And it came to pass, that in the morning watch the LORD looked unto the host of the Egyptians through the pillar of fire and of the cloud, and troubled the host of the Egyptians,

25 and took off their chariot wheels, that they drave them heavily: so that the Egyptians said, Let us flee from the face of Israel; for the LORD fighteth for them against the Egyptians.

26 And the LORD said unto Moses, Stretch out thine hand over the sea, that the waters may come again upon the Egyptians, upon their chariots, and upon their horsemen.

27 And Moses stretched forth his hand over the sea, and the sea returned to his strength when the morning appeared; and the Egyptians fled against it; and the LORD overthrew the Egyptians in the midst of the sea.

28 And the waters returned, and covered the chariots, and the horsemen, and all the host of Pharaoh that came into the sea after them; there remained not so much as one of them.

29 But the children of Israel walked upon dry land in the midst of the sea; and the waters were a wall unto them on their right hand, and on their left.

30 Thus the LORD saved Israel that day out of the hand of the Egyptians; and Israel saw the Egyptians dead upon the seashore.

31 And Israel saw that great work which the LORD did upon the Egyptians: and the people feared the LORD, and believed the LORD, and his servant Moses.

Exodus, Chapter 15:22-25, Bitter Water Made Sweet

22 So Moses brought Israel from the Red sea, and they went out into the wilderness of Shur; and they went three days in the wilderness, and found no water.

23 And when they came to Marah, they could not drink of the waters of Marah, for they were bitter: therefore the name of it was called Marah.

24 And the people murmured against Moses, saying, What shall we drink?

25 And he cried unto the LORD; and the LORD shewed him a tree, which when he had cast into the waters, the waters were made sweet: there he made for them a statute and an ordinance, and there he proved them,

1 Peter 3:20 Which sometime were disobedient, when once the longsuffering of God waited in the days of Noah, while the ark was a preparing, wherein few, that is, eight souls were saved by water.

Exodus 16:1-36, KJV

God Provided Manna (Bread) for the Children of Israel for Forty Years

1 And they took their journey from Elim, and all the congregation of the children of Israel came unto the wilderness of Sin, which is between Elim and Sinai, on the fifteenth day of the second month after their departing out of the land of Egypt.

2 And the whole congregation of the children of Israel murmured against Moses and Aaron in the wilderness:

3 And the children of Israel said unto them, Would to God we had died by the hand of the LORD in the land of Egypt, when we sat by the flesh pots, and when we did eat *bread* to the full; for ye have brought us forth into this wilderness, to kill this whole assembly with hunger.

4 Then said the LORD unto Moses, Behold, I will rain bread from heaven for you; and the people shall go out and gather a certain rate every day, that I may prove them, whether they will walk in MY law, or no.

5 And it shall come to pass, that on the sixth day they shall prepare that which they bring in; and it shall be twice as much as they gather daily.

6 And Moses and Aaron said unto all the children of Israel, At even, then ye shall know that the LORD hath brought you out from the land of Egypt:

7 And in the morning, then ye shall see the glory of the LORD; for that he heareth your murmurings against the LORD: and what are we, that ye murmur against us?

8 And Moses said, This shall be, when the LORD shall give you in the evening flesh to eat, and in the morning bread to the full; for that the LORD heareth your murmurings which ye murmur against him: and what are we? your murmurings are not against us, but against the LORD.

9 And Moses spake unto Aaron, Say unto all the congregation of the children of Israel, Come near before the LORD: for he hath heard your murmurings.

10 And it came to pass, as Aaron spake unto the whole congregation of the children of Israel, that they looked toward the wilderness, and, behold, the glory of the LORD appeared in the cloud.

11 And the LORD spake unto Moses, saying,

12 I have heard the murmurings of the children of Israel: speak unto them, saying, At even ye shall eat

flesh, and in the morning ye shall be filled with bread; and ye shall know that I am the LORD your God.

13 And it came to pass, that at even the quails came up, and covered the camp: and in the morning the dew lay round about the host.

14 And when the dew that lay was gone up, behold, upon the face of the wilderness there lay a small round thing, as small as the hoar frost on the ground.

15 And when the children of Israel saw it, they said one to another, It is manna: for they wist not what it was. And Moses said unto them, This is the bread which the LORD hath given you to eat.

16 This is the thing which the LORD hath commanded, Gather of it every man according to his eating, an omer for every man, according to the number of your persons; take ye every man for them which are in his tents.

17 And the children of Israel did so, and gathered, some more, some less.

18 And when they did mete it with an omer, he that gathered much had nothing over, and he that gathered little had no lack; they gathered every man according to his eating.

19 And Moses said, Let no man leave of it till the morning.

20 Notwithstanding they hearkened not unto Moses; but some of them left of it until the morning, and it bred worms, and stank: and Moses was wroth with them.

21 And they gathered it every morning, every man according to his eating: and when the sun waxed hot, it melted.

22 And it came to pass, that on the sixth day they gathered twice as much bread, two omers for one man: and all the rulers of the congregation came and told Moses.

23 And he said unto them, This is that which the LORD hath said, To morrow is the rest of the holy sabbath unto the LORD: bake that which ye will bake to day, and seethe that ye will seethe; and that which remaineth over lay up for you to be kept until the morning.

24 And they laid it up till the morning, as Moses bade: and it did not stink, neither was there any worm therein.

25 And Moses said, Eat that to day; for to day is a sabbath unto the LORD: to day ye shall not find it in the field.

26 Six days ye shall gather it; but on the seventh day, which is the sabbath, in it there shall be none.

27 And it came to pass, that there went out some of the people on the seventh day for to gather, and they found none.

28 And the LORD said unto Moses, How long refuse ye to keep MY commandments and MY laws?

29 See, for that the LORD hath given you the sabbath, therefore he giveth you on the sixth day the bread of two days; abide ye every man in his place, let no man go out of his place on the seventh day.

30 So the people rested on the seventh day.

31 And the house of Israel called the name thereof Manna: and it was like coriander seed, white; and the taste of it was like wafers made with honey.

32 And Moses said, This is the thing which the LORD commandeth, Fill an omer of it to be kept for your generations; that they may see the bread wherewith I have fed you in the wilderness, when I brought you forth from the land of Egypt.

33 And Moses said unto Aaron, Take a pot, and put an omer full of manna therein, and lay it up before the LORD, to be kept for your generations.

34 As the LORD commanded Moses, so Aaron laid it up before the Testimony, to be kept.

35 And the children of Israel did eat manna forty years, until they came to a land inhabited; they did eat manna, until they came unto the borders of the land of Canaan.

36 Now an omer is the tenth part of an ephah.

More on Bread in the Bible
Proverbs 4:17 – Bread is called the bread of wickedness.

17 For they eat the bread of wickedness, and drink the wine of violence.

1 Kings 17:1-6 King James Version (KJV)

1And Elijah the Tishbite, who was of the inhabitants of Gilead, said unto Ahab, As the LORD God of Israel liveth, before whom I stand, there shall not be dew nor rain these years, but according to MY word.

2 And the word of the LORD came unto him, saying,

3 Get thee hence, and turn thee eastward, and hide thyself by the brook Cherith, that is before Jordan.

4 And it shall be, that thou shalt drink of the brook; and I have commanded the ravens to feed thee there.

5 So he went and did according unto the word of the LORD: for he went and dwelt by the brook Cherith, that is before Jordan.

6 And the ravens brought him *bread* and flesh in the morning, and *bread* and flesh in the evening; and he drank of the brook.

Ecclesiastes 11:1 King James Version (KJV)

1 Cast thy *bread* upon the waters: for thou shalt find it after many days.

Matthew 4:3 King James Version (KJV)

3 And when the tempter came to Him, he said, If thou be the Son of God, command that these stones be made *bread*.

Matthew 4:4 King James Version (KJV)

4 But He answered and said, It is written, Man shall not live by *bread* alone, but by every word that proceedeth out of the mouth of God.

Matthew 6:11 King James Version (KJV)

11 Give us this day our daily *bread*.

John 6:35 King James Version (KJV)

35 And Jesus said unto them, I am the *bread* of life: he that cometh to Me shall never hunger; and he that believeth on Me shall never thirst.

Acts 27:35 King James Version (KJV)

35 And when He had thus spoken, He took *bread*, and gave thanks to God in presence of them all: and when He had broken it, He began to eat.

1 Corinthians 11:23-26 King James Version (KJV)

23 For I have received of the Lord that which also I delivered unto you, that the Lord Jesus the same night in which He was betrayed took *bread*:

24 And when He had given thanks, He brake it, and said, Take, eat: this is My body, which is broken for you: this do in remembrance of me.

John 6:41 King James Version (KJV)

41 The Jews then murmured at him, because He said, I am the *bread* which came down from heaven.

John 6:48 King James Version (KJV)

48 I am that *bread* of life.

49 Your fathers did eat manna in the wilderness, and are dead.

50 This is the *bread* which cometh down from heaven, that a man may eat thereof, and not die.

St. John 2:1-11, The Wedding At Cana

1 And the third day there was a marriage in Cana of Galilee; and the mother of Jesus was there:

2 And both Jesus was called, and his disciples, to the marriage.

3 And when they wanted wine, the mother of Jesus saith unto him, They have no wine.

4 Jesus saith unto her, Woman, what have I to do with thee? mine hour is not yet come.

5 His mother saith unto the servants, Whatsoever He saith unto you, do it.

6 And there were set there six waterpots of stone, after the manner of the purifying of the Jews, containing two or three firkins apiece.

7 Jesus saith unto them, Fill the waterpots with water. And they filled them up to the brim.

8 And He saith unto them, Draw out now, and bear unto the governor of the feast. And they bare it.

9 When the ruler of the feast had tasted the water that was made wine, and knew not whence it was: (but the

servants which drew the water knew;) the governor of the feast called the bridegroom,

The Beatitudes, Matthew 6:25-34King KJV

Matthew 6:25 Therefore I say unto you, Take no thought for your life, what ye shall eat, or what ye shall drink; nor yet for your body, what ye shall put on. Is not the life more than meat, and the body than raiment?

Matthew 6:26 Behold the fowls of the air: for they sow not, neither do they reap, nor gather into barns; yet your heavenly Father feedeth them. Are ye not much better than they?

Matthew 6:27 Which of you by taking thought can add one cubit unto his stature?

Matthew 6:28 And why take ye thought for raiment? Consider the lilies of the field, how they grow; they toil not, neither do they spin:

Matthew 6:29 And yet I say unto you, That even Solomon in all his glory was not arrayed like one of these.

Matthew 6:30 Wherefore, if God so clothe the grass of the field, which to day is, and to morrow is cast into the oven, shall He not much more clothe you, O ye of little faith?

Matthew 6:31 Therefore take no thought, saying, What shall we eat? or, What shall we drink? or, Wherewithal shall we be clothed?

Matthew 6:32 (For after all these things do the Gentiles seek:) for your heavenly Father knoweth that ye have need of all these things.

Matthew 6:33 But seek ye first the kingdom of God, and his righteousness; and all these things shall be added unto you.

Matthew 6:34 Take therefore no thought for the morrow: for the morrow shall take thought for the things of itself. Sufficient unto the day is the evil thereof.

Blood In the Bible

Leviticus 17:11 - For the life of the flesh [is] in the blood: and I have given it to you upon the altar to make an atonement for your souls: for it [is] the blood [that] maketh an atonement for the soul.

Hebrews 9:22 - And almost all things are by the law purged with blood; and without shedding of blood is no remission.

1 John 5:6 - This is He that came by water and blood, [even] Jesus Christ; not by water only, but by water

and blood. And it is the Spirit that beareth witness, because the Spirit is truth.

Hebrews 9:12-14 - Neither by the blood of goats and calves, but by His own blood He entered in once into the holy place, having obtained eternal redemption [for us]. For if the blood of bulls and of goats, and the ashes of an heifer sprinkling the unclean, sanctifieth to the purifying of the flesh: How much more shall the blood of Christ, who through the eternal Spirit offered himself without spot to God, purge your conscience from dead works to serve the living God?

Leviticus 17:14 - For [it is] the life of all flesh; the blood of it [is] for the life thereof: therefore I said unto the children of Israel, Ye shall eat the blood of no manner of flesh: for the life of all flesh [is] the blood thereof: whosoever eateth it shall be cut off.

1 Peter 1:19 - But with the precious blood of Christ, as of a lamb without blemish and without spot:

Hebrews 13:12 - Wherefore Jesus also, that He might sanctify the people with his own blood, suffered without the gate.

1 John 1:7 - But if we walk in the light, as He is in the light, we have fellowship one with another, and the blood of Jesus Christ his Son cleanseth us from all sin.

Ezekiel 16:6 - And when I passed by thee, and saw thee polluted in thine own blood, I said unto thee [when thou wast] in thy blood, Live; yea, I said unto thee [when thou wast] in thy blood, Live.

Genesis 9:4 - But flesh with the life thereof, [which is] the blood thereof, shall ye not eat.

Revelation 5:9 - And they sung a new song, saying, Thou art worthy to take the book, and to open the seals thereof: for thou wast slain, and hast redeemed us to God by thy blood out of every kindred, and tongue, and people, and nation;

Romans 5:9 - Much more then, being now justified by his blood, we shall be saved from wrath through him.

Leviticus 7:27 - Whatsoever soul [it be] that eateth any manner of blood, even that soul shall be cut off from his people.

Revelation 1:5 - And from Jesus Christ, [who is] the faithful witness, [and] the first begotten of the dead, and the prince of the kings of the earth. Unto him that loved us, and washed us from our sins in his own blood,

1 Peter 1:2 - Elect according to the foreknowledge of God the Father, through sanctification of the Spirit,

unto obedience and sprinkling of the blood of Jesus Christ: Grace unto you, and peace, be multiplied.

Acts 15:20 - But that we write unto them, that they abstain from pollutions of idols, and [from] fornication, and [from] things strangled, and [from] blood.

Hebrews 12:24 - And to Jesus the mediator of the new covenant, and to the blood of sprinkling, that speaketh better things than [that of] Abel.

Matthew 26:28 - For this is My blood of the new testament, which is shed for many for the remission of sins.

Psalm 72:14 - He shall redeem their soul from deceit and violence: and precious shall their blood be in his sight.

Matthew 16:14-17

14 And they said, Some say that thou art John the Baptist: some, Elias; and others, Jeremias, or one of the prophets.

15 He saith unto them, But whom say ye that I am?

16 And Simon Peter answered and said, Thou art the Christ, the Son of the living God.

17 And Jesus answered and said unto him, Blessed art thou, Simon Barjona: for flesh and blood hath not revealed it unto thee, but My Father which is in heaven.

18 And I say also unto thee, That thou art Peter, and upon this rock I will build My church; and the gates of hell shall not prevail against it.

Matthew 27:25 - Then answered all the people, and said, His blood be on us, and on our children.

Mark 14: 24 - And He said unto them, This is My blood of the new testament, which is shed for many.

Luke 22:44 - And being in an agony He prayed more earnestly: and his sweat was as it were great drops of blood falling down to the ground.

John 6:54 - Whoso eateth My flesh, and drinketh My blood, hath eternal life; and I will raise him up at the last day.

Mark 14:25 - Verily I say unto you, I will drink no more of the fruit of the vine, until that day that I drink it new in the kingdom of God.

1 Corinthians 11:25 –After the same manner also He took the cup, when He had supped, saying, this cup is the new testament in My blood: this do ye, as oft as ye drink it, in remembrance of me.

Ephesians 1:7 - In whom we have redemption through his blood, the forgiveness of sins, according to the riches of his grace;

1 Peter 1:19 - But with the precious blood of Christ, as of a lamb without blemish and without spot:

Revelation 12:11 - And they overcame him by the blood of the Lamb, and by the word of their testimony; and they loved not their lives unto the death.

Water In The Bible by Relevance (King James Version)

For Christians, water baptism exemplify the believer's total trust in, and total reliance on, the Lord Jesus Christ, as well as a commitment to live obediently to Him. Nicodemus said to Him, "How can a man be born when he is old? He cannot enter a second time into his mother's womb and be born, can he?" Jesus answered, "Truly, truly, I say to you, unless one is born of water and the Spirit he cannot enter into the kingdom of God. That which is born of the flesh is flesh, and that which is born of the Spirit is spirit. Do not be amazed that I said to you, 'You must be born again.' The wind blows where it wishes and you hear the sound of it, but do not know where it comes from and where it is going; so is everyone who is born of the Spirit." (John 3:4–8 KJV)

Acts 2:38 - Then Peter said unto them, Repent, and be baptized every one of you in the name of Jesus Christ for the remission of sins, and ye shall receive the gift of the Holy Ghost.

1 Peter 3:21 - The like figure whereunto [even] baptism doth also now save us (not the putting away of the filth of the flesh, but the answer of a good conscience toward God,) by the resurrection of Jesus Christ:

Matthew 3:11 - I indeed baptize you with water unto repentance: but he that cometh after me is mightier than I, whose shoes I am not worthy to bear: He shall baptize you with the Holy Ghost, and [with] fire:

Acts 22:16 - And now why tarriest thou? arise, and be baptized, and wash away thy sins, calling on the name of the Lord.

Mark 16:16 - He that believeth and is baptized shall be saved; but he that believeth not shall be damned.

Romans 6:4 - Therefore we are buried with him by baptism into death: that like as Christ was raised up from the dead by the glory of the Father, even so we also should walk in newness of life.

John 3:5 - Jesus answered, Verily, verily, I say unto thee, Except a man be born of water and [of] the Spirit, he cannot enter into the kingdom of God.

John 7:36-39

36 What manner of saying is this that He said, Ye shall seek Me, and shall not find Me: and where I am, thither ye cannot come?

37 In the last day, that great day of the feast, Jesus stood and cried, saying, If any man thirst, let him come unto Me, and drink.

38 He that believeth on Me, as the scripture hath said, out of his belly shall flow rivers of living water.

39 (But this spake he of the Spirit, which they that believe on Hm should receive: for the Holy Ghost was not yet given; because that Jesus was not yet glorified.)

John 19:34

34 But one of the soldiers with a spear pierced his side, and forthwith came there out blood and water.

Acts 10:48 - And He commanded them to be baptized in the name of the Lord. Then prayed they him to tarry certain days.

Galatians 3:27 - For as many of you as have been baptized into Christ have put on Christ.

Acts 8:36-39 -

36 And as they went on [their] way, they came unto a certain water: and the eunuch said, See, [here is] water; what doth hinder me to be baptized?

37 And Philip said, If thou believest with all thine heart, thou mayest. And he answered and said, I believe that Jesus Christ is the Son of God.

38 And he commanded the chariot to stand still: and they went down both into the water, both Philip and the eunuch; and he baptized him.

39 And when they were come up out of the water, the Spirit of the Lord caught away Philip, that the eunuch saw him no more: and he went on his way rejoicing.

Matthew 28:18-20 -

18 And Jesus came and spake unto them, saying, All power is given unto Me in heaven and in earth.

19 Go ye therefore, and teach all nations, baptizing them in the name of the Father, and of the Son, and of the Holy Ghost:

20 Teaching them to observe all things whatsoever I have commanded you: and, lo, I am with you always, [even] unto the end of the world. Amen.

Matthew 28:19 - Go ye therefore, and teach all nations, baptizing them in the name of the Father, and of the Son, and of the Holy Ghost:

Colossians 2:12 - Buried with him in baptism, wherein also ye are risen with [him] through the faith of the operation of God, who hath raised him from the dead.

Acts 2:41 - Then they that gladly received his word were baptized: and the same day there were added [unto them] about three thousand souls.

Matthew 3:16 - And Jesus, when he was baptized, went up straightway out of the water: and, lo, the heavens were opened unto him, and he saw the Spirit of God descending like a dove, and lighting upon Him:

Acts 10:47 - Can any man forbid water, that these should not be baptized, which have received the Holy Ghost as well as we?

Acts 8:38 - And he commanded the chariot to stand still: and they went down both into the water, both Philip and the eunuch; and he baptized him.

1 Corinthians 6:11 - And such were some of you: but ye are washed, but ye are sanctified, but ye are justified in the name of the Lord Jesus, and by the Spirit of our God.

Romans 6:3 - Know ye not, that so many of us as were baptized into Jesus Christ were baptized into his death?

Ephesians 5:26 That He might sanctify and cleanse it with the washing of water by the word

Isaiah 55:10-11

10 For as the rain cometh down, and the snow from heaven, and returneth not thither, but watereth the earth, and maketh it bring forth and bud, that it may give seed to the sower, and bread to the eater:

11 So shall My word be that goeth forth out of My mouth: it shall not return unto me void, but it shall accomplish that which I please, and it shall prosper in the thing whereto I sent it.

Hosea 6:3 Let us acknowledge the LORD; let us press on to acknowledge him. As surely as the sun rises, He will appear; He will come to us like the winter rains, like the spring rains that water the earth.

Amos 5:24 But let justice roll on like a river, righteousness like a never-failing stream!

The Crucifixion by Matthew, Mark, Luke & John

And finally in Matthew 27, verse 34, the soldier at the crucifixion of Jesus, with a spear pierces His side and water and blood came out.

The Crucifixion has been record in three places in the Bible: Matthew 27.32-50 · Mark15:21-37· Luke 23:26-49

Matthew 27:32-50

32 And as they came out, they found a man of Cyrene, Simon by name: him they compelled to bear his cross.

33 And when they were come unto a place called Golgotha, that is to say, a place of a skull,

34 They gave him vinegar to drink mingled with gall: and when He had tasted thereof, He would not drink.

35 And they crucified Him, and parted his garments, casting lots: that it might be fulfilled which was spoken by the prophet, They parted My garments among them, and upon My vesture did they cast lots.

36 And sitting down they watched Him there;

37 And set up over his head his accusation written, This Is Jesus The King Of The Jews.

38 Then were there two thieves crucified with Him, one on the right hand, and another on the left.

39 And they that passed by reviled him, wagging their heads,

40 And saying, Thou that destroyest the temple, and buildest it in three days, save thyself. If thou be the Son of God, come down from the cross.

41 Likewise also the chief priests mocking him, with the scribes and elders, said,

42 He saved others; Himself he cannot save. If He be the King of Israel, let Him now come down from the cross, and we will believe Him.

43 He trusted in God; let HIM deliver Him now, if HE will have Him: for He said, I am the Son of God.

44 The thieves also, which were crucified with Him, cast the same in his teeth.

45 Now from the sixth hour there was darkness over all the land unto the ninth hour.

46 And about the ninth hour Jesus cried with a loud voice, saying, Eli, Eli, lama sabachthani? that is to say, My God, My God, why hast thou forsaken me?

47 Some of them that stood there, when they heard that, said, This man calleth for Elias.

48 And straightway one of them ran, and took a spunge, and filled it with vinegar, and put it on a reed, and gave him to drink.

49 The rest said, Let be, let us see whether Elias will come to save him.

50 Jesus, when He had cried again with a loud voice, yielded up the ghost.

Mark 15:21-37

21 And they compel one Simon a Cyrenian, who passed by, coming out of the country, the father of Alexander and Rufus, to bear his cross.

22 And they bring him unto the place Golgotha, which is, being interpreted, The place of a skull.

23 And they gave him to drink wine mingled with myrrh: but He received it not.

24 And when they had crucified him, they parted his garments, casting lots upon them, what every man should take.

25 And it was the third hour, and they crucified him.

26 And the superscription of his accusation was written over, The King Of The Jews.

27 And with him they crucify two thieves; the one on his right hand, and the other on his left.

28 And the scripture was fulfilled, which saith, And he was numbered with the transgressors.

29 And they that passed by railed on him, wagging their heads, and saying, Ah, thou that destroyest the temple, and buildest it in three days,

30 Save thyself, and come down from the cross.

31 Likewise also the chief priests mocking said among themselves with the scribes, He saved others; Himself He cannot save.

32 Let Christ the King of Israel descend now from the cross, that we may see and believe. And they that were crucified with him reviled him.

33 And when the sixth hour was come, there was darkness over the whole land until the ninth hour.

34 And at the ninth hour Jesus cried with a loud voice, saying, Eloi, Eloi, lama sabachthani? which is, being interpreted, My God, My God, why hast thou forsaken me?

35 And some of them that stood by, when they heard it, said, Behold, He calleth Elias.

36 And one ran and filled a spunge full of vinegar, and put it on a reed, and gave him to drink, saying, Let alone; let us see whether Elias will come to take him down.

37 And Jesus cried with a loud voice, and gave up the ghost.

Luke 23:26-49

26 And as they led Him away, they laid hold upon one Simon, a Cyrenian, coming out of the country, and on Him they laid the cross, that he might bear it after Jesus.

27 And there followed Him a great company of people, and of women, which also bewailed and lamented him.

28 But Jesus turning unto them said, Daughters of Jerusalem, weep not for Me, but weep for yourselves, and for your children.

29 For, behold, the days are coming, in the which they shall say, Blessed are the barren, and the wombs that never bare, and the paps which never gave suck.

30 Then shall they begin to say to the mountains, Fall on us; and to the hills, Cover us.

31 For if they do these things in a green tree, what shall be done in the dry?

32 And there were also two other, malefactors, led with him to be put to death.

33 And when they were come to the place, which is called Calvary, there they crucified Him, and the malefactors, one on the right hand, and the other on the left.

34 Then said Jesus, Father, forgive them; for they know not what they do. And they parted his raiment, and cast lots.

35 And the people stood beholding. And the rulers also with them derided Him, saying, He saved others; let Him save Himself, if he be Christ, the chosen of God.

36 And the soldiers also mocked him, coming to Him, and offering Him vinegar,

37 And saying, If thou be the king of the Jews, save thyself.

38 And a superscription also was written over him in letters of Greek, and Latin, and Hebrew, This Is The King Of The Jews.

39 And one of the malefactors which were hanged railed on him, saying, If thou be Christ, save Thyself and us.

40 But the other answering rebuked Him, saying, Dost not thou fear God, seeing thou art in the same condemnation?

41 And we indeed justly; for we receive the due reward of our deeds: but this man hath done nothing amiss.

42 And he said unto Jesus, Lord, remember me when thou comest into thy kingdom.

43 And Jesus said unto him, Verily I say unto thee, Today shalt thou be with me in paradise.

44 And it was about the sixth hour, and there was a darkness over all the earth until the ninth hour.

45 And the sun was darkened, and the veil of the temple was rent in the midst.

46 And when Jesus had cried with a loud voice, He said, Father, into thy hands I commend My spirit: and having said thus, He gave up the ghost.

47 Now when the centurion saw what was done, he glorified God, saying, Certainly this was a righteous man.

48 And all the people that came together to that sight, beholding the things which were done, smote their breasts, and returned.

49 And all His acquaintance, and the women that followed Him from Galilee, stood afar off, beholding these things.

John 19:17-24 (What the soldiers did.)

17 And He bearing his cross went forth into a place called the place of a skull, which is called in the Hebrew Golgotha:

18 Where they crucified Him, and two others with Him, on either side one, and Jesus in the midst.

19 And Pilate wrote a title, and put it on the cross. And the writing was, JESUS OF NAZARETH THE KING OF THE JEWS.

20 This title then read many of the Jews; for the place where Jesus was crucified was nigh to the city: and it was written in Hebrew, and Greek, and Latin.

21 Then said the chief priests of the Jews to Pilate, Write not, The King of the Jews; but that he said, I am King of the Jews.

22 Pilate answered, What I have written I have written.

23 Then the soldiers, when they had crucified Jesus, took His garments, and made four parts, to every soldier a part; and also his coat: now the coat was without seam, woven from the top throughout.

24 They said therefore among themselves, Let us not rend it, but cast lots for it, whose it shall be: that the Scripture might be fulfilled, which saith, They parted My raiment among them, and for My vesture they did cast lots. These things therefore the soldiers did

25 Now there stood by the cross of Jesus His mother, and His mother's sister, Mary the wife of Cleophas, and Mary Magdalene.

26 When Jesus therefore saw His mother, and the disciple standing by, whom He loved, He saith unto His mother, Woman, behold thy Son!

27 Then saith He to the disciple, Behold Thy mother! And from that hour that disciple took her unto his own home.

28 After this, Jesus knowing that all things were now accomplished, that the Scripture might be fulfilled, saith, I thirst.

29 Now there was set a vessel full of vinegar: and they filled a sponge with vinegar, and put it upon hyssop, and put it to his mouth.

30 When Jesus therefore had received the vinegar, he said, It is finished: and he bowed his head, and gave up the ghost.

31 The Jews therefore, because it was the preparation, that the bodies should not remain upon the cross on the sabbath day, (for that sabbath day was a high day,) besought Pilate that their legs might be broken, and that they might be taken away.

32 Then came the soldiers, and brake the legs of the first, and of the other which was crucified with him.

33 But when they came to Jesus, and saw that He was dead already, they brake not his legs:

34 But one of the soldiers with a spear pierced His side, and forthwith came there out blood and water.

35 And he that saw it bare record, and his record is true; and he knoweth that he saith true, that ye might believe.

36 For these things were done, that the Scripture should be fulfilled, A bone of Him shall not be broken.

37 And again another Scripture saith, They shall look on Him whom they pierced.

The Bible and water, blood and bread are very much connected. Water is mentioned over 700 times in the scriptures. This is very interesting to me and may arouse your interest in reading more to learn more from the Bible.

The first time water is mentioned in the scripture is found in Genesis 1:2

Genesis 1:2 The earth was formless and empty, and darkness covered the deep waters. And the Spirit of God was hovering over the surface of the waters.

Before there was anything; light, sun or moon, earth, plants, living creatures or anything else, there was water.

Having created the earth out of water, and the sky in the midst of waters, and calling forth living creatures out of water, God continues to bathe his creation with water as a sign of His care.

The last time water is mentioned is in Revelations 22:17

Revelations 22:17 The Spirit and the bride say, "Come." Let anyone who hears this say, "Come." Let anyone who is thirsty come. Let anyone who desires drink freely from the water of life.

From Genesis to Revelations in the Bible, water flows throughout scriptures. Many passages link water to God's creation and the blessings of His chosen people. Water is important in our spiritual lives and Jesus tells us that. Jesus said, in John 4:13-14 (KJV):

> 13 Jesus answered and said unto her, Whosoever drinketh of this water shall thirst again:

14 But whosoever drinketh of the water that I shall give him shall never thirst; but the water that I shall give him shall be in him a well of water springing up into everlasting life.

Christians who believe in Christ Jesus should read, study, and meditate upon the Word of God. In Romans 12:2 KJV, the Bible says, "And be not conformed to this world but be ye transformed by the renewing of your mind, that ye may prove what is that good, and acceptable, and perfect, will of God."

Conclusion

In Chapter 5, I really wanted the reader to learn about Noah. God came to Noah with a request for him to build an Ark and what I like about Noah is that despite the naysayers and unbelievers, Noah was obedient and as a result he saved his family and many animals and he lived to be nine hundred and fifty years. I would like to think that I have also been obedient to God because when God revealed to me over 70 years ago about "Water Was Not Turned Into Wine," I knew I had to write about it, however, I also had naysayers. With this revelation and through a strong conviction I was determined to get the word out to as many people as possible about the evil of alcohol and strong drink. Many people in the world are suffering from alcoholism and it is destroying lives and families. I am hopeful "Water Not Turned Into Wine" will also convict the reader that Jesus Christ, according to scripture, did not turn water into wine, especially knowing all of the negative consequences of strong drink and the impact it would have on your life and your relationship with God.

In Chapter 6, "The Sermon on the Mount," Jesus, the master teacher, spoke to the multitudes and his disciples about how to live with each other. Many say that this is the greatest sermon Jesus ever preached. The Lord's Prayer, the beatitudes, and the golden rules are also in this sermon. I had to include this in my book because it also taught me how to live my life and treat others.

In my 96 years of living, I have had many shares of trials and tribulations. From a very young age, I've had to provide for my family and it was very hard. I lost my brother at a young age. I lost my mother after she lived a full life. I lost one of my grandchildren at tender age of 20 in a tragic accident. I've been very ill and thought I was going to die from Malaria. Most recently, I lost my wife of nearly 71 years and we lived a wonderful life together. By the same token, I have been blessed to have six children and have lived to see them grow up and have families of their own. With life's ups and downs God has always been by my side and I will never forsake him.

In conclusion, from a young boy, I discovered that the Bible was indeed a sacred Holy Book which has taught me many valuable lessons about how to live a good Christian life on a daily basis. I would encourage the readers of "Water Not Turned Into Wine" to search and study the Bible as I did, and then apply those lessons in your life and become "Spirit-led" so you too can discover other truths about Christ's teaching as I did some seventy years ago. It is very important to become a life-long student of the Bible who is not ashamed, and who rightly divides the words of truth so as to "err not" in interpreting passages from the Bible, because you will suffer for lack of this knowledge.

I have included some more of my favorite verses and parables for your enrichment, however, there is so much more for you to study. Here are just a few more:

Matthew 7:16 Ye shall know them by their fruits. Do men gather grapes of thorns, or figs of thistles?

Matthew 7:17 Even so every good tree bringeth forth good fruit; but a corrupt tree bringeth forth evil fruit.

Matthew 7:18 A good tree cannot bring forth evil fruit, neither can a corrupt tree bring forth good fruit.

Matthew 7:19 Every tree that bringeth not forth good fruit is hewn down, and cast into the fire.

Matthew 7:20 Wherefore by their fruits ye shall know them.

Matthew 4:19 And He saith unto them, Follow me, and I will make you fishers of men.

Matthew 4:4 But he answered and said, It is written, Man shall not live by bread alone, but by every word that proceedeth out of the mouth of God.

What fruit will you bear as you go through life? Will you be a fisher of men or will your seeds be thrown on rocks and reap no fruit? Here is an assignment for you, read all of Matthew, in particular, Matthew 5:1-14 and then the rest of the Bible. Maybe, God has something to reveal to you. God bless everyone who read "Water Not Turned Into Wine." I hope it will inspire you to rethink drinking all forms of "strong drink," and choose a non-alcoholic drink instead. Well like Noah, I have been obedient and by spreading the word about water was not turned into wine at the "Wedding at Cana" and I hope I have saved my family and other lives from this evil mocker.

In Psalms 90, verse 10, it states, "The days of our years are threescore years and ten; and if by reason of strength they be fourscore years, yet is their strength labour and sorrow; for it is soon cut off, and we fly away. In Biblical days this was considered to be seventy years or eighty years or the span of a life. I have been blessed to live 94 years, which is fourscore and fourteen. This is proof of a life lived well for God through Christ and the biblical teachings. You too can live such a life if you abide by words of the Bible, trust in the Lord with all you heart and soul. Also like Noah and Job, I have lived a long life and when God is ready for me, I will "fly away," because I will have fulfilled what God has put upon my heart to do by writing "Water Not Turned Into Wine." I believe God allowed me to live this long, because He must have another purpose for me. I did not want to go to my grave without quoting these scriptures so it could help the world.

The Bible teaches the following about a living sacrifice and a sober mind in Romans 12:1-21, "1 I beseech you therefore, brethren, by the mercies of God, that ye present your bodies a living sacrifice, holy, acceptable unto God, which is your reasonable service. 2 And be not conformed to this world: but be ye transformed by the renewing of your mind, that ye may prove what is that good, and acceptable, and perfect, will of God. 3 For I say, through the grace given unto me, to every man that is among you, not to think of himself more highly than he ought to think; but to think soberly, according as God hath dealt to every man the measure of faith."

Jesus said, in John 4:14, "But whosoever drinketh of the water that I shall give him shall never thirst; but the water that I shall give him shall be in him a well of water springing up into everlasting life. Jesus has quenched my thirst all of these years. I hope you will also drink the water of everlasting life.

Finally the Bible says, Let your light so shine before men, that they may see your good works, and glorify your Father which is in heaven. Matthew 5:16 I hope my light continues to shine before men who see my good works and that I have glorified my Father which is in heaven. The Bible teaches in Revelation 22:19, that, "And if any man shall take away from the words of the book of this prophecy, God shall take away his part out of the book of life, and out of the holy city, and from the things which are written in this book. (Revelation 22:19 KJV) AMEN

If this book has touched you in a special way, http://henrylouisgreen191.wix.com/hlgproductions and share how it has impacted your life through an email to henrylouis.green1919@aol.com and add me as a friend on Facebook.

THE BEGINNING

He who began a good work in you will be faithful to complete it until the day of Christ Jesus.
Philippians 1:6

Henry Louis Green's Auto-Biography

Early Years

I was born March 30, 1919, in South Boston, Va. I was born of a mixed relationship which at the time was taboo. I was the youngest child of Ida Green and a White man named William Glenn. William Glenn fathered three children with Ida Green, one boy, myself and two girls, Mary and Bessie. My father, William, has been described as good hearted, intelligent, hard working and to his detriment; he loved "colored people, in particular, Ida." While William was very much in love and wanted to marry Ida, his parents would not allow it. In defiance, William and Ida went to Philadelphia and stayed almost two years. However, his mother thought he was crazy for wanting to marry a colored woman, so she had him committed to the infamous Western

State Lunatic Asylum, Staunton, VA., until his death at age 70. My mother, Ida raised me and my siblings (3-brothers Johnnie, Joseph, Thomas and 4 sisters-Mildred, Bessie, Ida Frances, and Mary (who was actually my cousin) as best she could as a single parent. My mother wanted to settle down with someone, however, the men in her life only stayed around two or three years and then moved on. Times were hard, especially during the Depression. As a young boy, I did whatever I could to care for and feed my mother's family. My younger brother, Thomas died of pneumonia when he was only 2 years old. I remembers seeing Thomas watching the trains go by and saying, "White Man, Yellow Man, Black Man," before he became sick. The death of Thomas motivated me to take on more responsibility and I became the man of the house at age 13.

I preferred reading Aesop Fables, such as "The Old Man, The Boy and The Donkey", because it had a moral to the story and I learned valuable lessons from it, like you can't please all the people all the time. I did not like the primer books that taught nursery rhymes, such as "The Cow Jumped over the Moon" and the story of Santa Claus or Easter Bunny because they were confusing to me as child and then later I learned they were lies and I felt betrayed by the adults in my life. I guess because I had to grow up so fast, I had no time for fairy tales and nursery rhymes that didn't teach me anything about life. So you see the man I am today is because the Bible and the sayings of Jesus are the rock of my salvation and the foundation which I built my understanding about how to live my life.

The Bible says, "Trust in the Lord with all your heart, And lean not on your own understanding; In all your ways acknowledge Him, And He shall direct your paths" (Proverbs 3:5,6). The Bible also teaches, "Put not your trust in princes, nor in the son of man, in whom there is no help." (Psalm 146:3)

I love to swim. I learned to swim at an early age and swam as smoothly as Johnny Weissmuller, the original Tarzan. I learned my farming skills from my grandfather, Henry Green, Sr. ("Papa") on my mother's side of the family and my White grandfather, Sam Glenn on my father's side of the family. Being half white or a mulatto, as they were called back in the day, I lived in two worlds, loved by some and resented by others. My grandfather, managed Sam Glenn's farm and I went to work with him every day and played with the children of the sharecroppers. I remember being raised mostly by my Grandfather, Henry, Sr. My mother was very busy with my siblings. I attended school until the 4th grade and then dropped out of school to support my mother and siblings.

Courtship

Since I had helped to raise my siblings, by age 21, it was time for me to start my own family. I met Marion Henderson in South Boston. I believed that of the three eligible women in the neighborhood, Marion was the prettiest. I believe Marion was attracted to me because of my fair skin color and wavy black hair. We courted in front of the fireplace at Marion's parent's house. The courtship was short and we married on December 23, 1939, two days before Christmas. We were married at the courthouse before a Justice of the Peace. Marion paid $7.00 for her dress (one weeks pay) and $1.98 for her shoes. I wore my work clothes. After the ceremony, we both went back to work so there was no honeymoon. I was 21 and Marion was 16, however, she said she was 18 on the marriage license.

Marriage

Our first-born was Robert Henry, then Lorenzo Lewis, Priscilla Lee, Ted William, Cynthia Bernice (deceased before one year due to neglect at the hospital during labor), Serita Bernice, and Carroll Brent.

We lived on a farm in the early years, raising pigs, cows, and chickens and we grew most of our food. Marion didn't know how to cook at first so I purchased a cook book. Marion learned quickly the art of cooking. When Marion wanted to make clothes I got her a sewing machine. Marion became a wonderful seamstress and made most of her children's clothes and clothes for herself.

Childrearing

We were both very spiritual and raised our children using biblical principles. "Spare the rod, spoil the child." Like many couples, we disagreed on discipline. I was very strict and used biblical principle, "spare the rod spoil the child," however Marion preferred to use her strong words to get things done. We joined the Memorial Baptist Church in South Boston, Va. Where they both sang in the choir and made sure their children attended church every Sunday.

Career/Education/Community Involvement

Determined to make a better life for my family, I commuted back and forth to Washington, D.C. for five years, coming home every other week-end. I bought many used cars and some of them were very unique including a Studebaker and a hearse. Marion stayed home and raised the children. They were difficult years. The house was at the dead-end (fondly called "the bottom") of a road; however, there was another house nearby that sold liquor and one night Marion heard someone outside the house late at night. So being the strong women she was, she took my 45 gun out, loaded it, and went on the porch and shot it into the air. They never heard from that intruder again. In 1964, I moved my family to Washington, D.C. I believed that our children would have a better life in the city.

Although I dropped out of school at an early age, as an adult, I returned to school and received my GED. Marion attended school until the 9th grade and then dropped out because she was embarrassed for not having enough clothes. I worked in various jobs in the Washington Metropolitan area and eventually began a career with the United Planning Organization (UPO). I worked at UPO almost 25 years. I believe I made significant contribution to the organization receiving many awards including certificates from the former Mayor of D.C., Marion Barry for my landscaping skills. I was the first in the Washington, D.C. area to supervise and teach landscaping to inner city youth in the Job Corp program.

While working in the UPO Neighborhood Youth Corp (NYC), I taught many young men about the wisdom of life, as well as the basics of landscaping. My work can be seen if one drives down Beach Drive in Rock Creek Park, and also the Meridian Hill Park on 16th Street NW, Washington, DC.

After I left the NYC, I was promoted to the position of Job Placement Specialist. Recently, I was recognized for my years with the Job Corp program and a new project was developed and appropriately named, "The Henry L. Green Parks Maintenance Project." In 2009, a grant from Washington Convention Center was awarded to the Shaw Ministries for the establishment of a landscape and maintenance project. The project will train Shaw residents landscaping basics and maintenance. My youth program was the pilot program for job development and placement.

The Golden Years

Marion and I were truly blessed to have experienced our Golden Years for quite some time. It was our children, grand-children, and great-grand-children that kept us feeling young and very active. I currently reside in Mitchellville, Md. Today, at age 93, I continue to enjoy gardening. When Marion was in good health we would drive all the way to D.C.'s Tubman Elementary School to get food from the Mid-Atlantic Gleaning Network and the Capital Area Food Bank, and then deliver the food to our neighbors, friends, and especially those who are widows. I have completed three books that are ready for publishing and I'm thinking about launching a recording career. I have a total of 6 children, 16 grandchildren, and 16 great-grandchildren and two great-great grandchild. I lost my wife, Marion on June 21, 2011. Although Marion is absent in the physical sense, I continue to give love, support, advice, counsel and encouragement to all of our family and friends. I would like to inspire others by being an example of helping others. I believe that a wise man will seek out good counsel to become enlightened. A wise man will hear, and will increase learning; and a man of understanding shall attain unto wise counsels. Proverbs 1:5

As I've said, I raised my children using biblical principles and as you can see from their biographies they exemplify the results of what the Bible says, "Train up a child in the way he should go: and when he is old, he will not depart from it." (Proverbs 22:6 (KJV))

Introduction of the Children by Ted William Green (Third Son)

I'd like to introduce myself. I'm Ted William Green. Third son and the older middle child among six born to Henry L. and Marion H. Green. I'm so very proud and thankful of the way I was raised. Some of the principles embedded in us as children can be better understood as to who we are by referencing the below listed quotes, statements and biblical terms:

1. Always remember that you are better than no one, but also remember that no one is better than you.

2. Treat others as you wish to be treated

3. Do your share and not just your part

4. A bird in the hand is worth more than two in the bush

5. God, family, country

6. are the company that you keep

7. Remember Christ in the days of your youth

8. Honesty is the best policy

9. Do what you wish, however do so in moderation

10. Love thy neighbor as thyself

11. You can take a horse to the well, but you can't make him drink

12. Early to bed and early to rise makes you healthy, wealthy and wise

13. The same moon and sun are shared worldwide

We were raised as a close knit sharing family and remain one today because of our parents and what they stood for. Both were hardworking and dedicated, and both returned to school as adults to get their high school diploma or equivalency. By some standards we were poor, but I would not exchange the experiences of my upbringing for neither silver nor gold. After reading this brief synopsis you should be able to recognize who my parents, my siblings and myself are and from my father's point of view by using those principles above plus the Bible, he and my mother raised responsible and upstanding citizens.

Henry and Marion Green Children

Their first born, Robert Henry Green, was born on September 7, 1940 in South Boston, Va. He graduated from Bethune High School in 1959 and in the U.S. Navy from 1960-1964 and served as a Radar Man 3rd Class. He worked in the field of Electronics and Engineering for over 25 years, for such companies as Honeywell, RCA, GE, MIT, Lincoln Labs and he worked with Head Start for 15 years. He graduated from the University of Rhode Island with a Bachelors degree in Science, Human Development and Family Study. His other experience and interest as musician and guitarist, he opened for Dizzy Gillespie, 1980, Boston, MA. He is a Solar Energy Engineer and has received a U.S. Patent on a "Solar Collector System," 2013. He is also the founder of Early Literacy Program, "Reading Kingdoms" (www.readingkingdoms.org).

Their second oldest son, Lorenzo Louis Green was born, September 23, 1942, in South Boston, Va. He attended Mary Bethune High School, and afterwards like his older brother Robert, Lorenzo served in the U.S. Navy from 1962 to 1966, as a Ship Serviceman Barber with the ranking of E3. After being discharged from the Navy honorably, he wanted to be a D.C. policeman; however, I suggested that he go to school for cosmetology. He graduated from Calvinade Beauty Academy, in Washington, D.C., in 1968. The Director of Calvinade recommended him to Johnson's Product Company, a company educating hairdressers on the use of its products. He worked at several local salons before opening up his own salon called, Lorenzo's of Halifax in Washington, D.C. He is now a certified instructor or Sr. Cosmetologist. With over 53 years of experience, he is currently writing an educational book on the business of hair styling and designs, which also includes how to sell and promote the business side of cosmetology, and how customers can determine if they have received the proper services. Lorenzo is currently working as a Cosmetologist in Upper Marlboro, MD. His interests also include writing poetry, one of which was well received by President Barack Obama, entitled, "Tomorrow, Tomorrow, Tomorrow." He also enjoys painting landscapes and abstract art and is the Orator on the album, "The Vision" produced by The Virginia Sons of Harmony (insert year). On that album Lorenzo recites a narration entitled, "Free At Last" which is his rendition of Dr. Martin Luther King's speech, "I Have A Dream."

Their oldest daughter, Priscilla (Lee) Green Francis was born in South Boston, Halifax Co, VA on November 9, 1943. Priscilla graduated from Mary Bethune High School in 1962. After relocating to Washington, DC, she accepted a job at the National Institutes of Health and attended Strayer College at night. In the 1970's and 80's, she attended Howard Community College. During the 1990's, she enrolled in business administration courses at Howard University earning her Certificate as a Certified Community Action Professional (C-CAP). In 1966, she was fortunate enough to secure employment with The United Planning Organization, Inc. (UPO), Neighborhood Development Center # 1 (NDC #1) as a clerk typist gaining respect, promotion and admiration from the very start. Over the past 32 years, Priscilla has worked tireless with UPO/NDC # 1 to improve the living conditions, community outlook and quality of life for residents of the District and the Shaw Community in particular. Before retiring from UPO in 2010, she worked with the Foster Grandparent Program. Even though she is retired she is still on the board of several affiliations, including the Thurgood Marshall Center for Service and Heritage. In retirement, she turned her love of connecting clients with resources; that in turn, empower families to live better lives into a non-profit organization, called Resources Plus. Anyone who has spent any amount of time with Priscilla knows she loves the Lord by her words and deeds. She was born again in Christ in 1978 and is a member Crossover Church in Hyattsville, MD. Priscilla loves singing and music and sings in the choir at Crossover, She is often be found participating in a multitude of church activities.

My third son, Ted William Green, was born May 7, 1946. Ted graduated from Bethune High School and followed in the footsteps of his brothers by doing a tour in the Navy from 1964 - 1968 as a Ship's Serviceman. Ted graduated from the University of Maryland in May, 1995 with a degree in Business and technology. He also earned a recent degree in Computer

Science from Montgomery College. Ted has had a career of over 30 years as a professional in the District Government in his field of study. He has also worked as a Information Systems consultant in private industry. Ted has traveled to over 20 countries among them are Serbia, Turkey, Hungary, Croatia, Germany, England, Cuba, Austria, Canada, Panama, Macedonia, Greece, Cuba and many others in the Caribbean.

Their fifth child, Serita (Bernice) Green Newell, was born in South Boston, Halifax County, VA on August 1, 1952. Serita moved with her parents to Washington, D.C. when she was 10. She matriculated through the District of Columbia school system and graduated from Theodore Roosevelt High School, in 1970. She worked several years in the private industry before entering into the Federal government in 1975, at the Interstate Commerce Commission. While in the Federal government, Serita received a Certificate of Paralegal Studies from the University of Maryland University College. She continued her career as a Paralegal Specialist at the Federal Deposit Insurance Corporation until she retired in 2002 after 28 years. Upon retirement, she became a full-time mother. She also participated in various business adventures with her husband, Larry W. Newell and assisted with the care of her parents. Most recently, she was instrumental in the publication of her husband's novel, Chronic In America and her father's soon to be published book, Water Was Not Turned into Wine. She is a member of First Baptist Church of Glenarden in Upper Marlboro, MD.

Their sixth and youngest son, Carroll Brent Green, was born August 26, 1956, in South Boston, Halifax County, Va. He matriculated through the school systems in Virginia and Washington, D.C. and ultimately graduated from Boston High School, in 1974 in Boston, MA. Brent pursued a career in electronics, getting a certificate in electronic engineering from Lincoln Tech. He worked in that field for many years. He has a home-based business repairing household items. Most recently, he along with his sister, Priscilla, have been the primary care-givers of their father, Henry Louis Green.

ORIGINAL EXCERPTS FROM MANUSCRIPT

The following are excerpts from Henry's
original hand-written manuscripts.

INSPIRATION   Good NAme
UNDERSTANING   ~~Seek midwife~~
CHARACTER   ~~POOR~~

SAVE - Few loaves Bread & Fish

② These Are VALUES I Learn from Searchen
The Scriptures, and applying them to my daily life.
Jeremiah 29:13. Verse.
And ye shall seek me, and find me, when ye shall search
for me with all your heart.

① IN My Life Growing up at an early age
Going Forward with The Future
And Looking back in Time with the Past.

234

His mother SAITH UNTO The servant, whatsoever
He saith UNTO you. do iT.

wine

FiLL The WATER pots. With WATER

AND THey Filled Them up To The brim

when The Ruler ~~Had~~ of The

~~FEAST~~ HAD TASTED ~~WATER~~ . THE

WATER .

AND KNEW NOT WHENCE IT WAS

BUT THE SERVANTS WHICH Drew

The WATER KNEW.

The ~~Rul~~ Governor Call The

The WATER WINE

AND KNEW NOT when iT was

The SeRVANTS WAS The only ones

Knew. Then JESUS SAID UNTO Them, FiLL The

WATERpots WITH WATER — AND they Filled Them up

To The brim.   over ⟶

It's The woman at the well, the water
that would give, she would never thirst again.
for the time.

it was wine — But the future
drink, was so much different he
Just called it ~~good~~ wine.
To go along with the program,
But did not know what it was.
The servant knew. And they were
the only one that knew. Except
Jesus. Because he told them
To Fill the water pots with
water. And thats what they did.
And Thats ~~while~~ the mother (of Jesus)
told them, The servent—
To Do what he said da.

236

GOD's Holy Bible Says This, About Wine

Numbers 6 Chapter Verse: 1-2-3-4

AND The LORD spake unto Moses, Saying,
Speak unto The children of Israel, and say unto
Them, when either MAN or woman Shall separate
Themselves To Vow a Vow of a Nazarite, To separate
Themselves unto The LORD:
He Shall separate himself from Wine and strong
drink, and shall drink No Vinegar of Wine, or Vinegar
of strong drink, neither shall he drink any liquor
of grapes, Nor eat moist grapes or dried.
All the days of his separation shall he eat
Nothing that is made of the Vine Tree, from the
kernels even To The husk.

Luke 1 Chapter Verse 13-14-15

But The angel said unto him, Fear Not, Zach-a-ri-as:
for Thy prayer is heard; and thy Wife Elisabeth Shall bear
Thee a son, and thou shalt Call his Name John.
And Thou shalt have Joy and gladness; and many shall
Rejoice at his birth.
For he shall be great in the sight of the Lord, and
shall drink neither Wine nor strong drink;
and he shall be filled with Holy Gost,
even from his mother's womb -
And many of The childrens of Israel shall he Turn/
To The Lord Their God.

John 2

Water was not turn to wine

1 John 2

2 And the third day there was a marryiage in "Cana of
2 Galilee; and the mother of Jesus was there:

2 And both Jesus was called, and his disciples,
   to the marriage.

3 And when they wanted wine, the mother
   of Jesus saith unto him, They have no wine.

4 Jesus saith unto her, Woman, what have i to
   do with thee? mine houre is not yet come.

5 His mother saith unto the servants, whatsoever
   he saith unto you, do it.

6 And there were set there six waterpots of
   stone, 'after the manner of the purifying
   of the Jews, containing two or three
   firkins a piece.

7 Jesus saith unto them, Fill
   the waterpits with water.
   And they filled them up to the brim.

8 And he saith unto them, Draw out now, bear
   unto the governor of the feast.
   And they bare it.

9 When the Ruler of the feast had tasted
   the water that was made wine,
   and knew not whence it was:
   but the servants which drew the
   water knew:) the Governor of the
   feast called the bridegroom.

10 And saith unto him, Every man at the
   beginning doth set forth good wine; <
   and when men have well drunk then that
   which is worse: but thou has kept the
   the good wine until now.

A Good Name Reather To be Called than Riches - Prov 22:1 21

WOMAN At the well TALKING to Christ

who is your NABOR

WALKING ON THE WATER

PEARCE IN the Side out came WATER & BLOOD Luke 23:5

CARRING the Cross - NAIL To the Cross Three on the Cross 5
John 19:17

PIOLET & Christ TALKING who CALLED The (KING)
who

whom do MEN's SAY that I Am Christ ASK disiple

HE with out A FAULT CAST the first STONE

WATCH while I PRAY Jesus Ask his Discipes.

Peter AND the Cock CROWING

JohN BAPTISING,

DOVE LIT ON Christ Shoulder - WhasIng Feet

(Your GOD is My God - Where you Lode I will Lodeg
A DoughTER IN LAW TALKING mother iN LAW)

Chech the SCRIPTUERS out.

OLD MAN BEAR & Childrens,   To see
                                            Of Christ
Sickermore FARtree Zickerisea Climed up   coming by

Seaman Fishing Cast Net ON The other Side
                                    catch men
Sower went Fore To Sow Seed

SERMAN ON TH MOUNT   And
What will a man To gain the World Lose his Soul

Remember the CREATOR iN days of youth,

PURE RELING AND UNFILE befoe DOD

                    WRIT THIS ON A Clean PAAy
HERE ARE SOME MORE OF GOD;S WORD TO HELP
WALK IN THE LIGHT THAT OTHERS MAY SEE YOUR
Good WORKS AND GLORY GOD.
                    AND GIVE YOU MORE
                            UNSTNING;

239

✓

St. John 2 Chapter verses

9   When the Ruler of the feast had tasted
    the water that was made wine,
    and knew not whence it was:
    But the servants; which drew the water knew;

St. Matthew 26 - Ch - Ver 26
26 And as they were eating Jesus took Bread and
    blessed it and brake it and gave to the disciples
    and said, Take, eat, this is my body.
27 And he took the cup, and gave thanks, and gave
    it to them saying, Drink ye all of it for this is
28 my blood of the New testament, which is shed
    for many for the Remission of sin.
29 But I say unto you, I will not drink henceforth
    of this fruit of the vine, until that day when
    I drink it new with you in my fathers Kingdom.
30

WATER

PS 23:2 beside the still water.
He maketh me to lie down in green
pastures: he leadeth me beside the
still waters.

854

prov 25:21 water to a thirsty soul
if thine enemy be hungry, give him bread
to eat; and if he be thirsty, give him
water to drink:

861

Eccl 11:1 bread upon the water
Cast thy bread upon the waters:
for thou shalt find it after many days.

874

a well of living water song 4:15
A fountain of gardens, a well of living waters,
and streams from Leb-a-non.

922

Is 43:2 passeth through the water
when thou passest through the waters, I will be
with thee; and through the rivers, they shall
overflow thee: when thou walkest throug
thee; thou shalt not be burned; neither shall
flame kindle upon thee.

(WATER)

IS 55:1 Come ye to the Water ! 936 4/13
To every

Jer 2:13 Fountain of living Water 949

Matt 3:11 baptize you with living Water 1199
I indeed baptize you with water unto Repentance:
but he that cometh after me is mightier than I, whose
Shoes I am not worthy to bear: he shall baptize you
with the Holy Gost, and with fire:

Matt 10:42 a cup of Cold Water 1210
And whosoever shall give to drink unto one of
these little ones a cup of cold water only in the name of
a disciple, verily I say unto you he shall in no wise lose his Reward.

John 1:26 I baptize with Water 1326
John answered them, saying, I baptize with water:
but there standeth one among you, whom ye know
not:

John 7:38 Rivers of living Water 1338
He that believeth on me, as the scripture hath said,
out of his belly shall flow Rivers of living Water.

Rev 22:17 take the Water of life 1566
and The spirit and the bride say, Come, and let him That
heareth say Come, and let him That is athirst come.
And whosoever will, let him Take the Water of life freely.

to Marriage Wine Page 1327 John Chapter 2 Book (Page 1566)

Revelation 22:9

22:19 And if any man shall take away from the words of the book of this prophecy God shall take away his part out of the book of life, and out of holy city, and from the things which are written in this book.

it New in the Kingdom of God

BLOOD

~/13

PS 72:14 precious shall their blood
He shall Redeem their soul from deceit and
violence: precious shall blood be in his sight. ✓

Matt 16:17 flesh and blood.
He saith unto them, But whom say ye that I am?
and Simon Peter   and said, Thou art the the Christ,
the son of the Living God.
MATT 27:25 His blood be on us.
Then answered all the peoples, and said, His blood
be on us and on our childrens. ✓

MARK 14:24 blood of the New Testament
And he said unto them, This is my blood of the new
Testament, which is shed for many.

Luke 22:44 great drops of blood

John 6:54 drinketh my blood ✓

____ of valor . com

MATT 14:28 Verily I say unto you, I will not drink
No more of the fruit of the vine until that day that I drink

BREAD

1 KIN 17:6 Ravens brought Bread

eccl 11:1 Cast thy Bread

matt. 4:3 Stone be made Bread

MATT 4:4 Shall Not Live by bread

matt 6:11 this day our daily Bread

John 6:35 I am the Bread of Life

$56-$60 wholesale
$3.45 - sling box   1 Peter 5:17

References

1. "Author Completes Book After 70 Years of Writing," Author Unknown, The Gazette, August 29, 2013

2. Office of the Surgeon General. (2007). The Surgeon General's Call to Action To Prevent and Reduce Underage Drinking (PDF 1.41MB) Rockville, MD: U.S. Department of Health and Human Services.

3. Office of the Surgeon General. (2007). The Surgeon General's Call to Action To Prevent and Reduce Underage Drinking: A Guide for Families (PDF 900KB) Rockville, MD: U.S. Department of Health and Human Services.

4. U.S. Department of Health and Human Services, Substance Abuse and Mental Health Services Administration. Reach Out Now Teach-In Lesson Plan.

5. Statistics are from The United States Depart of Justice, Office of Justice Programs, Office of Juvenile Justice and Delinquency Pre-prevention, http://www.udetc.org/documents/Drinking_in_America.pdf-(Updated in 2002)

6. Pilgrimage to the Holy Land: The Marriage at Cana, http://www.stjudechapel.org/pilgrimage-to-the-holy-land-the-marriage-at-cana/, 2/1/2013

7. Steubenville, weary of investigation, faces new probe, by Michael Pearson, CNN, updated 10:05 PM EDT, Mon March 18, 2013 http://www.cnn.com/2013/03/18/justice/ohio-steubenville-case/index.html

8. Teen fatally shot entering neighbor's home in N.Va., The Associated Press, March 18, 2013, http://hamptonroads.com/2013/03/teen-fatally-shot-entering-neighbors-home-nva

9. Augustine, Saint, Hippo, Quaestiones in Heptateuchum, 2, 73: PL 34, 623, On The Relationship Between the Old and the New Testament, Retrieved August 20, 2015, Bible Junkies.com: http://www.biblejunkies.com/2013/09/on-relationship-between-old-and-new.html

10. Rummelsburg, Steven Jonathan, St. Agustine's Commentary on the Sermon on the Mount, 2014. Retrieved August 20, 2015 from Crisis Magazine.com: http://www.crisismagazine.com/2014/st-augustines-commentary-on-the-sermon-on-the-mount

Other Sources

For more information on the effect of alcohol on the body please go to these websites:

http://lifehacker.com/5684996/what-alcohol-actually-does-to-your-brain-and-body

http://science.howstuffworks.com/life/inside-the-mind/human-brain/alcoholism4.htm

http://faculty.washington.edu/chudler/alco.html

http://www.youtube.com/watch?v=zXjANz9r5F0 (Alcohol and Your Brain)

http://en.wikipedia.org/wiki/Long-term_effects_of_alcohol

Notation:

Whenever the word "LORD" in all caps or small caps appears in the Old Testament, it is a replacement for when God's original Hebrew text name "YHWH," pronounced Yahweh, appears. It is known as the Tetragrammaton. The Tetragrammaton consists of the four letters YHWH forming the sacred name of the supreme Deity of the Ancient Hebrews. The Jerusalem Bible uses the name, Yahweh, throughout. In the editor's foreword of the Jerusalem Bible, it states that to not use the accurate form of HIS translated name, "would be to lose much of the flavour and meaning of the originals." Therefore, in the King James version of the Bible, LORD God refers to God Yahweh (YHWH, the tetragrammaton). When the Bible used the word "Lord", in this format it is referring to Jesus. When you see "lord", in this format it is referring to a prophet or master. Also, out of reverence for God and the Christ, I civilize, the pronouns for God and Christ Jesus.

Also, in the King James Version (KJV of the Bible, words of Jesus are in red. In reverence to Christ Jesus, all references to Him and God, as pronouns should be capitalized. If I have inadvertently missed doing that, please forgive me.

Printed in the United States
By Bookmasters